# Blessed Are the Peacemakers

## TEN STEPS TO PEACE

Mary E. Latela

Liguori
ONE LIGUORI DRIVE
LIGUORI MO 63057-9999

Imprimi Potest:
Richard Thibodeau, C.Ss.R.
Provincial, Denver Province
The Redemptorists

ISBN 0-7648-0960-1
Library of Congress Catalog Number: 2002112208

© 2003, Mary E. Latela
Printed in the United States of America
03 04 05 06 07   5 4 3 2 1

Scripture quotations are from the *New Revised Standard Version of the Bible,* © 1989 by the Division of Christian Education of the National Council of the Churches of Christ in the USA. Used by permission. All rights reserved.

To order, call 1-800-325-9521
www.liguori.org
www.catholicbooksonline.com

# Contents

# Dedication

∽

To Annette and Paul,
Robert and Ann,
Cathy and Walter,
with love and gratitude!

# Introduction

The message on my answering machine was an invitation. My dear friends, Marge and David, said, "We're having some friends over. Come, bring something to share for supper and something to share in the circle…a song, a story, a poem."

We gathered on that Saturday evening, some old friends, some new. The potluck meal was wonderful, working out as these things do: always enough—more than enough—and a variety of tastes and textures. The table was decorated with purple flowers, orchids and cosmos, and many candles.

After the meal, we went into the cozy living room, and I was asked to play the piano, "Let There Be Peace on Earth, and Let It Begin with Me." We each lit a candle, one of eighteen candles—separate yet melted together. David helped us to focus by leading a centering meditation, and then the sharing began. Someone who'd worked in the rescue efforts in Fairfield County, Connecticut, told about an amazing connection that helped to personalize the tragedies of 9-11. Another person shared an inspirational e-mail about the change in our perspective before and after that day, another read a poem she'd written, another shared a quiet hope for community.

An amazing woman who dedicated her life to spreading a message of peace by traveling around the United States and Canada wrote of her "pilgrimage":

> Never underestimate the power of a loosely knit group working for a good cause. All of us who work for peace together, all of us who pray for peace together, are a small minority, but a powerful spiritual fellowship. Our power is beyond our numbers.
>
> PEACE PILGRIM[1]

As I looked around the room at our little peace gathering, peering into the faces of these people who had come to share, I understood that the search for peace is poly-cultural, multifaith, intergenerational, and open to all. Peace begins in one person's heart, and then in another, and before you know it, it's a powerful movement.

# 1

# Make Peace With Yourself

## WATCH OUT FOR THE SECOND ARROW

*Scriptural Focus* ~ *Matthew 6:25-34; Philippians 4:4-9*

Thich Nhat Hahn is a Buddhist teacher and writer. In a presentation he called "Living Happily, Dying Peacefully," Nhat Hahn talked about "the second arrow." If a person were to be shot with an arrow, that would be very painful, of course. But, he asked, if a person were to be shot with a *second* arrow in the very same spot, would the pain be twice as much? No! The pain would be much, much more intense.

The Buddhist said that the first arrow is our pain, whether physical, emotional, or spiritual, whether a family problem or a problem with work or with our community. The second arrow is the fear, the worry, the anger, the frustration, which we add to the pain. So, Thich Nhat Hahn says, "Watch out for the second arrow!"

This really resonates with me, for I know that I sometimes add to my challenges with a tendency to worry or become afraid, thereby multiplying my angst. How do we avoid the second arrow without denying the real pain, suffering, and confusion we have? I believe it involves a process wherein, little by little, we learn to let go of the stuff that we've added on. This process begins with the hope, trust, and expectation that God is with us always. God is with us in the sunshine and in the rain, in the darkness and in the light. God is still with us when the world seems frightening and when life seems to be turned upside-down.

Did you ever have a friend who would support you during a difficult time, someone you could call at any hour—day or night—who would always have time to listen and help? We have not only our human friends. We have a Brother and Teacher who walks with us everywhere.

Try to imagine Jesus walking with you. He gently, yet firmly, holds your hand. You walk along the beach. You can smell the salty air. You can feel the spray of sea water. You look out upon the ocean and, as far as your eyes can see, there appear to be diamonds sparkling on the surface of the water.

As you walk together, clouds race across the sky—dark clouds, angry clouds—and the wind picks up and hurts your face. It starts to rain, a cold hard rain, and the waves begin to crash upon the shore. You begin to feel afraid. You wonder what will happen to you.

Then you look over, and you know that Jesus is still holding firmly onto your hand. If you become really frightened and begin to panic, and even feel as if your might die, Jesus puts his strong arm around your shoulder, like a big brother.

You can bury your face in his shoulder and you know you are safe.

And after a while the sea is calm again, and you *are* safe. You know, too, that anytime you want to, you can return to this time and place, this strong presence of Jesus walking along with you, no matter where life takes you.

*Watch out for the second arrow.* If you really do reduce your anxiety, will your problems magically disappear? No. However, you will not be using up precious energy that can be diverted to positive actions. You can begin to explore what to do. You can ask yourself: What do I need? Who can help me? How can I solve my problems? How can I reduce my suffering?

The horrible events of September 11, 2001, profoundly reminded us that we are not a disparate mob of individual persons wandering the world in despair. We are all connected. When another person rejoices, we all rejoice. When another person suffers, we all suffer. We have seen that people need people, that we can and do help one another in ways that are tangible and in ways that are not.

Many of us lit candles, attended prayer services, connected with family and friends, huddled together to keep warm and safe. We are now, as a nation, in a time of transition—a time of possibilities and of challenges. We hope and pray that the evil which came into our lives can be dispelled with compassion and peaceful negotiation.

We fear that more lives may be sacrificed in this quest for peace. But the worst thing we can do is to sit at home, doors locked, afraid to go out, afraid to read the papers. The worst thing we can do is to allow our caution to become panic, our concerns to become paralyzing anxiety.

If we are discouraged, that is normal. If we are tired, that is OK. If we are angry, confused, frustrated, worried, that is to be expected. If we feel as if we have experienced a death, that is not surprising. We are all dealing with loss. The loss is different for each of us, to be sure, but the grief is real. And the good news is that grieving isn't stagnant; it moves along...to a better place, somewhere down the road.

～

I was in ministry at a small church in North Dakota when floods ravaged the lands. We had to deal with the aftermath. Many people found that the phenomenon of the floods sent them back, mentally and emotionally, to an earlier time when they had felt similar pain or similar helplessness. And this has happened here and now, as people deal with the aftermath of that assault on civility and peace in New York City and in Washington, D.C.

We may be drawn back to other times when we were vulnerable. For some, the powerful memories of World War II may be recurring, or Vietnam, or the Gulf War. Others may be reliving some personal trauma—the death of a spouse or other loved one, or loss of a precious relationship. We may be feeling again some old grief that we thought had healed, but which is reopened by the present stress. This happens. But how do we deal with this vulnerability, this feeling of helplessness, this need to be on the defensive? How do we work through this, so that we can move on without getting caught up in fear and anxiety, even terror?

I think that the early disciples of Jesus had to do this after Jesus was gone. They reached back into their memories for times when Jesus was there to heal them, to take away their fears, to stop the winds and the waters, to calm the storm. This connection with the Lord certainly doesn't erase whatever we're struggling with, but it may very well help us in our healing process, and every healing is a process.

Prayer is our connection with God. We are invited to talk all this over with God. Some of us talk a great deal, others use few words. It doesn't matter. Have you noticed how people who have been friends for a long time, or couples who have been married many years, don't need to use a lot of words? They can just be together in silence, often for hours, and it's OK. We can do this with God. If we want to talk on and on, God will listen. And if we want to be silent—and part of the time we really *ought* to be silent—we can simply be there, in the presence of God, and listen and enjoy.

People still ask, why should we talk to God when God already knows what we need? Friend, God doesn't need our prayer. But *we* need it. We need to talk to God and listen to God. Prayer can help to clarify what we are feeling, what we need, what we want. Jesus urged us to pray daily, for our "daily bread," for whatever we need. He promised that whatever we need will be provided abundantly, in overwhelming amounts. We pray both for our own good and to deepen our relationship with God. Sometimes we find that our prayer changes over time. God hasn't changed, perhaps the situation hasn't changed, but our attitude changes, or our perspective changes.

Scripture reminds us that there is nothing so small or so trivial that God does not care about it. God is concerned with sparrows and lilies and grains of sand and the stars and the sea. Of course, God cares about you and me. God cares that we are grieving and hurting. God cares that most of us are puzzling over the events of 9-11, and that we're concerned about what is happening in our world.

God is not the source of our worry or fear or anxiety, those secondary sources of suffering that multiply our pain, but God can help us with those things. Two women remind us of that:

> A weary Christian lay awake one night trying to hold the world together by his worrying. Then he heard the Lord gently say to him, "Now you go to sleep, Jim; I'll sit up."

RUTH GRAHAM BELL[2]

> There are two golden days in the week, upon which, and about which, I never worry—two carefree days, kept sacredly free from fear and apprehension.

> One of these days is Yesterday; yesterday, with its cares and frets, all its pains and aches, all its faults, its mistakes and blunders, has passed forever beyond my recall....It was mine! It is God's.

> The other day that I do not worry about is Tomorrow; tomorrow, with all its possible adversities, its burdens, its perils, its large promise and poor performance, its failures and mistakes, is as far beyond my mastery as...Yesterday....Tomorrow is God's day! It will be mine!

> There is left for myself, then, but one day in the week—Today. Any man can fight the battles of Today! Any woman can carry the burdens of just one

day! Any man can resist the temptations of today!…it is when we willfully add the burdens of those two awful eternities—Yesterday and Tomorrow—that we break down. It isn't the experience of Today that drives [us] mad. It is the remorse for something that happened Yesterday; the dread of what Tomorrow may disclose.

These are God's days! Leave them with Him!

MRS. CHARLES COWMAN[3]

One of the strongest obstacles to being at peace, to remaining calm and confident, is our *perception* that we are all alone in our struggles. We are *not* alone. Our lives are interlaced with all humanity, our well-being is shared with all creation. We are here to help one another.

A flight of sparrows swoops into a bush near the bird feeder. From there, they fly to the feeder and to the ground below to collect the seed. Each bird stays near the others. They come in together. They go out together. There is no leader. There are no words spoken. At the feeder, it seems each bird is in it for itself, but in flight, the group mind takes over. It feels better to fly in with the group and take off with the group. Being alone in the big yard makes a sparrow nervous. Sparrows know there is safety in the flock. They don't reflect upon it, perhaps, as we might, but they feel it and react accordingly.

Humans like to think of ourselves as independent, but we benefit from closeness and connection with others. We are part of a group mind. Rather than individuals cut off from each other and not mattering in the scheme of things, we are each part of something bigger than ourselves. Our simple expression of kindness may save a life that saves another life that changes the world.

TOM BARRETT[4]

*Our simple expression of kindness may save a life that saves another life that changes the world.*

Remember that whatever you suffer, you are not alone. God is near; God is in your heart. Your brothers and sisters, all of God's other children, are near. Watch out for the second arrow—the worry, the fear, the anxiety—and if you feel it coming, ask for help.

Sometimes, we have to cling to small hopes.

*Why worry or be uptight?*

*If you are hurried, you can slow down;*
*If you are late, you can miss something;*
*If you miss something,*
      *then you didn't have it to do,*
*You can do something else, if you want.*
*You can apologize, make amends for being late.*

*If you are hurt, you can heal;*
*If you are tired, you can rest;*
*If you are empty, you can fill up;*
*If you are sad, you can cry;*
*If you are lonely; you can be with someone;*

*If you hate, you can forgive;*
*If you are weak, you can pray.*

*You are as you are.*
*Life is as it is.*

*Join it.*
*Be a part of it—just as it is.*
*Be natural.*
*You are provided for.[5]*

### Step 1: *Make peace with yourself!*

Therefore I tell you, do not worry about your life, what you will eat or what you will drink, or about your body, what you will wear. Is not life more than food, and the body more than clothing? Look at the birds of the air; they neither sow nor reap nor gather into barns, and yet your heavenly Father feeds them. Are you not of more value than they? And can any of you by worrying add a single hour to your span of life? And why do you worry about clothing? Consider the lilies of the field, how they grow; they neither toil nor spin, yet I tell you, even Solomon in all his glory was not clothed like one of these. But if God so clothes the grass of the field, which is alive today and tomorrow is thrown into the oven, will he not much more clothe you—you of little faith? Therefore do not worry, saying, "What will we eat?" or "What will we drink?" or "What will we wear?" For it is the Gentiles who strive for all these things; and indeed your heavenly Father knows that you need all these things. But strive first for the kingdom of God and his righteousness, and all these things will be given to you as well.

So do not worry about tomorrow, for tomorrow will bring worries of its own. Today's trouble is enough for today.

MATTHEW 6:25-34

Rejoice in the Lord always; again I will say, Rejoice. Let your gentleness be known to everyone. The Lord is near. Do not worry about anything, but in everything by prayer and supplication with thanksgiving let your requests be made known to God. And the peace of God, which surpasses all understanding, will guard your hearts and your minds in Christ Jesus.

Finally, beloved, whatever is true, whatever is honorable, whatever is just, whatever is pure, whatever is pleasing, whatever is commendable, if there is any excellence and if there is anything worthy of praise, think about these things. Keep on doing the things that you have learned and received and heard and seen in me, and the God of peace will be with you.

PHILIPPIANS 4:4-9

# 2

# Be at Peace

## A Day in the Life...

*Scriptural Focus* ~ *Mark 6:30-34,53-56*

A young man had lost his job and didn't know which way to turn. He went to see his grandmother. Pacing about his grandmother's parlor, the young man clenched his fists and cried: "I've begged God to help me. Tell me, Grandma, why doesn't God answer?" The wise old woman spoke something in reply, something so hushed it could not be heard.

The young man stepped across the room. "What did you say?" he asked. The old woman repeated herself, but again in a voice as soft as a whisper. So the young man moved closer, until he was leaning on the arm of his grandmother's chair. "Sorry," he said, "I still didn't hear you."

With their heads bent together, the grandmother spoke once more. "God sometimes whispers," she said, "so that we will come near and listen more closely." And the young man understood.

Consider a typical day in the life of Jesus of Nazareth. Jesus went off with his disciples for a time of prayer and silence. Then they went into the crowds, where Jesus was teaching and healing. These two pieces seem to contrast activity with silence, action with contemplation. In the life of Jesus, these were interwoven as carefully as the strands of a fine rug. On a regular basis, Jesus went off to spend some time alone, in prayer and silence, until it was time to go out and attend to the crowds again.

There is no doubt about it, Jesus of Nazareth was a very busy person. And he certainly sensed that his ministry had a real urgency about it. He must have known that his radical message would upset the status quo and, in time, he would be condemned. And yet, Jesus led an incredibly balanced life. He only began his public ministry at the age of thirty, when the time was right. And he never gave in to the temptation to rush from place to place to do more and more.

People throughout the ages have become busy with their lives. You and I are very busy. How do we do everything we need to do and still keep a balance? How do we attend to all our responsibilities without becoming exhausted or sick? It really is a challenge. Even in summertime, when so many are vacationing, there is a temptation to fill up the leisure hours with almost frenzied activity. If we look carefully at a day in the life of Jesus, I think we can pick up some pointers about being focused, even when we have a lot to do.

First of all, Jesus took the time to share meals with his friends; indeed, sometimes with his adversaries (although these might be considered "business lunches"). Jesus had a demanding schedule. He was a teacher, and this, as some of you know from your own experience, was a tremendous responsibility. Jesus was a healer. Most people in the healing professions work long hours and have to make decisions quickly and surely, often life and death decisions. Jesus worked with people, but he also satisfied his need for silence and time alone.

He was always gracious to those who approached him kindly, yet he wasn't afraid to confront those were only out to test him or to criticize the company he kept. He did not waste time with them. Jesus was interrupted in his work. Like many busy people (new parents, for example), he'd begin a task and then get called away to something else—and when it was all over, he would often have to referee an argument among his disciples.

How did he keep his focus? We could say that Jesus was special, so he must have had an extraordinary ability to keep things going. But we need to see Jesus as truly human, susceptible to the same frustrations as we are. He got tired. He dealt with people who were just plain annoying. There was a lot of noise. He was on the road much of the time, without the comfort of a warm place called home. And he had a vocation that was very difficult. He came not only to teach by his words, but by his life. He taught people that the most important lessons are to love God and to love our neighbor as ourselves. And he lived out that message himself.

It seems clear that Jesus drew strength for his work from God, his Father. To be a healing presence to others requires prayer and reflection. Jesus had a regular pattern of prayer and reflection time. Often, he went out into the night to pray, and he spent a long time, hours, in that manner. And he kept that serenity in his heart when he was working with the people.

When I think about how the everyday life of Jesus compares to my own life, I see that I need to prioritize. I need to keep a balance of work and rest and time with family and friends. I need to focus on what I am doing right now, without worrying too much about all that is left to do, and without wasting energy trying to redo the past. I take to heart the advice of a contemporary writer, who suggests that we need to give up the hope of a better past in order to be happy now.

I am aware that I need to keep my connection with God. I absolutely must spend time in prayer and silence, in just being quiet, listening for "the still, small voice" of the Lord. I need to ask God to keep me in balance. When we are in balance, we pursue our goals, but we are not overwhelmed with disappointment if our plans fail. When we are in balance, we see that life is good, and we understand that bad times are only temporary. We understand that inconvenience is part of life, and life is not always fair.

We move on emotionally from our losses, and we share our gains. Every one of us is also called to be attentive to God's presence in our lives at each moment. Mindfulness is a way of focusing on the productive thoughts and feelings, and minimizing the distractions. It simply means being aware, not only when we are alone, but also in the busy times, and especially in our interactions with other people.

When we think about how Jesus acted toward others, we see that he was truly in the moment. Jesus listened attentively to those who came to him. He looked at those who came to him, actually looked into their hearts, and this was frightening for some, who knew what they thought they were hiding. We are called to really look at and really listen to the people in our lives. That is our highest priority.

Jesus reached out to people with a healing touch, people who were marginalized because of purity laws that declared that the sick and women and others were "ritually unclean" and not to be touched. When some people brought their sick friends and family members to Jesus for healing, Jesus gently approached them, looked intently at them, and laid his hands upon them and healed them.

We are challenged to be gentle with others, and to be a healing presence for them. If we are tempted to think of Jesus as too good to be true (or real), we have evidence that he was *very* real. He had genuine feelings for people, and he expressed righteous anger, and he showed disappointment when his message was rejected. Near the end of his ministry, he lamented. *"Jerusalem, Jerusalem, the city that kills the prophets and stones those who are sent to it! How often have I desired to gather your children together as a hen gathers her brood under her wings, and you were not willing!"* (Matthew 23:37).

We can be real, too. We can express our honest feelings, both of joy and of disappointment, and know that we are not alone. Did you know that people who are serene are naturally more compassionate? There is a strong connection between a calm spirit and a loving heart.

Have you noticed that your capacity to feel and express love is inversely related to the level of tension in your mind and body? When we are problem solving and working on survival issues, the higher order emotions, such as love and compassion, tend to get squeezed out of consciousness. Our instinct to survive is basic, and when physical survival was the main occupation of human persons, they learned to be on heightened alert all the time. So now when we feel anxious, we use the flight or fight response, and our mind becomes narrowly focused on the problem at hand.

TOM BARRETT[6]

Being open to silence, to patience, to compassion, requires resolve and perseverance. Sometimes it's easier, even more exciting, to worry and to focus on problems. On the other hand, in calmness our hearts can open to love, generosity, and compassion.

Love does not thrive when we are very tense, when we are driving on the Interstate to work or rushing to a meeting, even to Sunday worship, or when we are afraid or very tired. Sometimes it is tempting to seek the "adrenaline rush" to keep us awake and invigorated. We enjoy the lift of observing something "breathtaking." But as a steady diet, "breathtaking" can leave us irritable and lonely.

Instead, we can practice entering a calmer, more peaceful state of being, even for a short period of time each day. When we sit calmly in the silence, our senses become more refined, our appreciation of beauty deepens, and we can't help being more loving and more receptive to love.

I once read about a famous surgeon who decided that, in order to have time with God, he would have to get up very early. So he did. And it made a difference in his life. You and I know people who are not famous or important in the eyes of the world, but who make sacrifices—getting up before the family is up, or making adjustments in their professional life —in order to make a sacred space for God. It's simply what people do in order to stay close to the Lord, and this is in spite of the warning about what can happen when we decide to build silence into our days. "We need silence in our lives. We even desire it. But when we enter into silence we encounter a lot of inner noises, often so disturbing that a busy and distracting life seems preferable to a time of silence" (Henri Nouwen).[7]

So we have to keep at it. When we consider a day in the life of Jesus, we can find some help for our own spiritual life. As the wise woman told her grandson, we need to lean into God in order to listen and to hear. If we desire peace, we take time to cultivate peace. We breathe in peace. We breathe out all our fears and concerns. We release unneeded tension. We wait in silence. We listen. In the calm, we grow strong. In strength, we grow kind. We live in beauty. And love shines in our hearts and spills over to our brothers and sisters, all the children of God.

## Step 2: Be at peace!

> The apostles gathered around Jesus, and told him all that they had done and taught. He said to them, "Come away to a deserted place all by yourselves and rest a while." For many were coming and going, and they had no leisure even to eat. And they went away in the boat to a deserted place by themselves. Now many saw them going and recognized them, and they hurried there on foot from all the towns and arrived ahead of them. As he went ashore, he saw a great crowd; and he had compassion for them, because they were like sheep without a shepherd; and he began to teach them many things.

MARK 6:30-34

When they had crossed over, they came to land at Gennesaret and moored the boat. When they got out of the boat, people at once recognized him, and rushed about that whole region and began to bring the sick on mats to wherever they heard he was. And wherever he went, into villages or cities or farms, they laid the sick in the marketplaces, and begged him that they might touch even the fringe of his cloak; and all who touched it were healed.

MARK 6:53-56

# 3

# Make Peace
# With God

## THE SOURCE OF PEACE

*Scriptural Focus* ∼ *Psalm 23*

W e may be hesitant to "make peace with God" because of the misperception that we are not "right with God." This is not only an inaccurate view, but it can harm us; it can hold us back from an awareness of our unshakeable bond with the very Source of all Being. God is our Creator, after all, and God loves us unconditionally. God is the Source of Peace. When we feel confused, anxious, worried, or alone, we may run away from the very One who can help us.

Where do we look for God? We don't have to leave our homes, leave even the chair on which we are sitting, to find God. Jesus said—and it is central to his teaching—"*the kingdom of God is among you*" (Luke 17:21b).

This does not mean that you or I are gods, that we are

all-powerful, omnipresent, to be idolized or worshiped. Rather, it means that the grace, the love, the power we seek from God is not somewhere else—not in some faraway place, not even limited to churches and other places of worship. God places, within you and me, the kingdom. And what is the kingdom? It is the place where God dwells.

> Your true address is: body, mind, united here and now. You don't need any zip code.
>
> It is also the address of God. It is the address of the Kingdom of God, it is the address of our ancestors, all our beloved ones are there. The address of love. The address of compassion. The address of freedom, also. I have arrived, I am home…your true home is in the here and the now.
>
> THICH NHAT HANH[8]

I heard a man tell his own story of experiencing re-connection with the Lord. I will never forget the passion and love with which he recounted his journey. When he was a child, his parents taught the love of God in their home. He went to church with his family. He attended Sunday School faithfully. He was even a Youth Leader. And he proclaimed Jesus as his Lord and Savior. He was a believer.

But something happened to that early faith. The man was tempted by drugs, and he did succumb. His body was filled with chemicals, but his heart was empty. He was so lonely that he almost despaired. He was driving aimlessly along a deserted road, came to a fork in the road, and decided to go one way and not the other. And before too long, his car ran out of gas in front of a church, a seemingly abandoned church.

Afterwards, he took that as a sign. At the time, he just sat in his car, and cried and cried. He felt like such a failure. He was overcome with feeling bad about himself, and about life, and about God. He was convinced that God would not want to have anything to do with him.

Then, his eyes filled with tears, he stumbled into that church, and he knew that the Lord was there all the time, waiting for him. And he knew it wasn't the building, but the presence of the Lord, that changed his heart. And he was a new person, carrying the Christ-love within him everywhere.

Today, that man is a pastor, and a wonderful preacher who humbly recounts this story to celebrate the truth that God forgives…even him…even you and me. At the core of our reflections on our disconnectedness with God is the amazing truth that God has forgiven each of us, so many times. When we fail, we know that we can turn to God in repentance and be assured of forgiveness. "Anyone in Christ becomes a new person altogether; the past is finished and gone, everything has become fresh and new. Friends, hear and believe the good news: In Jesus Christ we are forgiven."[9]

﹏

When we are dealing with a major struggle, a serious health concern, the aftermath of a national tragedy, we may wonder where God was when we were hurting. How could God allow such pain and suffering? How could God allow thousands of people to be killed, and millions to be forever changed? We may decide that it's better not to have anything to do with such a God than to live with situations that have no simple answers.

I think God understands that we are going through a phase in our grief, that we will hope again. God doesn't stop pouring out grace and courage and perseverance just because we are confused. God waits. And in time, we usually do move through our grieving, our doubting, and our uncertainty.

About six weeks after 9-11, I read in a periodical that America had moved on from disbelief to anger. I assume that the writer was sincere in the personal observation that grieving is a natural and progressive process. However, grieving is not a neat package, with each stage completed before moving on to the next and, within a short time, acceptance. I was disturbed by this lack of understanding. Those of us who have suffered loss in the past know that grieving is *not* a tidy process.

Disbelief/anger/depression/confusion/acceptance overlap; we may take a couple of steps forward, then move back. We can't say, "OK, that's enough grieving. Time to move on. It's not patriotic to still be angry."

Even when we reach some level of acceptance of the situation, it is not static. Events may come up which cause us to relive the pain: an anniversary, a similar tragedy, a personal problem that "seems" to be unrelated. There are some pains that never go away. I like to say that this pain rests in my heart, and once in a while I take it out and cry about it. And I am not alone, because God is with me and in me and around me…and never stops caring about my pain…and will sit with me as long as I need that special presence.

"Survivor guilt" is not an affliction limited to those who escape death or trauma. Sometimes people actually feel apologetic that they are OK while others, who seemed to be heroes, did not survive. Such judgments, which usually reflect an unrealistic self-image, are not healthy. You and I are here, now. What will we do with the life we have to honor our Creator, to use our gifts to love one another, and to care for all that God has entrusted to our care?

If we feel a little disconnected from God, what better time to realize that and ask God for help? God does not hold grudges. God will not remind us of some past error which will never be forgiven.

God is all about acceptance and love and communion… starting with you and me.

### Step 3: Make peace with God!

*The LORD is my shepherd, I shall not want.*
*    He makes me lie down in green pastures;*
*he leads me beside still waters;*
*    he restores my soul.*
*He leads me in right paths*
*    for his name's sake.*
*Even though I walk through the darkest valley,*
*    I fear no evil;*
*for you are with me;*
*    your rod and your staff—*
*    they comfort me.*
*You prepare a table before me*
*    in the presence of my enemies;*

*you anoint my head with oil;*
*    my cup overflows.*
*Surely goodness and mercy shall follow me*
*    all the days of my life,*
*and I shall dwell in the house of the* LORD
*    my whole life long.*

PSALM 23

# 4

# Make Peace With the Past

## FORGIVENESS

*Scriptural Focus* ∼ *Genesis 50:15-21; Matthew 18:21-22*

In Spain, the story is told of a father and his teenage son who had a relationship that had become strained. So the son ran away from home. His father began a journey in search of his rebellious son. Finally, in Madrid, in a last desperate effort to find him, the father put an ad in the newspaper. The ad read: "Dear Paco, meet me in front of the newspaper office at noon. All is forgiven. I love you. Your father."

The next day at noon, in front of the newspaper office, eight hundred "Pacos" showed up. They were all seeking forgiveness and love from their fathers.

JAMES S. HEWETT[10]

Can you remember that magical moment where despair begins to blossom into hope? Or that quiet moment when a little bit of light comes into a very dark place? Some of us know what it's like to undergo the pain of the prodigal—knowing that we have failed and feeling as if we are dying, yet wanting so much to believe in forgiveness. And then forgiveness comes, like a welcome rain on a parched summer day.

Daily, we make choices that lead us to either connect with God or wear down that connection. If we are sorry, we confess to God, and we are forgiven. If we have committed a public sin, then we are required to seek out the brother or sister whom we have offended, and walk with them to God. God can change our heart, if we want that.

We can cooperate with *metanoia* by being open and honest with God. After all, every kind action we choose makes our life and the lives of all human persons better, and every hateful thought or action diminishes all humankind.

If someone does wrong to me, must I forgive? should I? can I? may I? If I forgive too easily, am I setting myself up to remain a victim? The problem of the unrepentant sinner is difficult, because there is not even a request for forgiveness. At first glance, it seems like cheap grace. What do we do with a life *filled* with hateful thoughts and actions, a hard attitude of intolerance so thick that the child of God is barely visible in the person? What do we do with collective guilt, where decisions have been made which resulted in nations and races suffering horribly and the damage seems irreparable?

We have recently heard leaders of faith communities and leaders of nations apologize for past horrors. Their words may fail to convince unless accompanied by concrete, immediate, and consistent changes in acting. As individuals and as communities, we need to understand that shame is not the same as repentance. Repentance requires a commitment to do whatever we can to make amends. I think it's obvious that confessing "just a little bit" does not relieve us of responsibility, and the harm done cannot be erased by a few well-chosen words. There must be power behind the words, there must be an acknowledgment of the enormity of the guilt. There must be a commitment to new ways of thinking and acting—so that never again...*never again*...will such pervasive evil occur.

↶

Near the end of the Book of Genesis, the brothers of Joseph, who had long before pawned him off as a slave, recognize him. And they are terrified. They fear that Joseph will take revenge upon them. They know they have done a terrible thing, an act that has altered the history of their family and seriously hurt their father Jacob. They *expect* Joseph to retaliate. But he doesn't. Against all odds, he embraces his brothers and forgives them.

Simon Peter comes to Jesus and asks him, "How many times must we forgive?" How many times are we expected to forgive someone who has offended us and who shows no sign of repenting? Are we supposed to forgive someone who has hurt us so deeply that we know we will never be the same? I think we can assume that Peter was annoyed by the behavior of someone else, and was getting tired of forgiving him or her. And Jesus' answer challenges Peter's sense of justice. How many times? Not seven, but "seventy-seven times"!

When there is no acknowledgment of wrongdoing,

should we forgive? After all, the offenders don't seem to even be sorry. They seem to be thriving, and we are still suffering because they hurt us.

No, we are not required to, but we may gradually reach a point where we *want* to forgive—to let go of the wrong, so that we can move on with life, so that our energy will be spent on healthy issues instead of our exhaustive efforts to stay estranged from the offending person.

If I refuse to forgive someone who has hurt me, I am allowing myself to be controlled by the other person. I continue to struggle with that other. I waste energy. This is a struggle that is not healthy for me.

Let's be clear. We are never supposed to condone bad behavior. We are not meant to stay involved with people who repeatedly hurt us. Forgiving does not require forgetting, and it does not require us to accept abusive behavior. But when it can happen, reconciliation is sweet. The truth is that the forgiving person benefits the most.

I heard a memorable sermon some years ago. The preacher offered the question, "What are you holding on to? Who has offended you so badly that you are still preoccupied with them? Chances are, the other person either is not aware that you are still hurting or does not even care. Move on with your life and let go of the insult that you still carry in your heart. It can make you ill."

When someone has done us wrong, we have a choice. We can hang on to the hurt forever—and we all know people who *have*, not speaking to each other for decades at a time— or we can get rid of the hurt by asking God to lift the burden. Until we are ready to forgive, we are stuck with our anger. That anger may be directed at someone else, but *it lives in us.*

When we cling to anger, it is as if we set ourselves on fire in order to burn someone else. Forgiveness is an act of the will and an act of healing. It *may* heal the one who wronged us. It *may* heal the relationship. It *will* heal our own wounded heart.

> *Forgiveness is an act of the will and an act of healing. It* may *heal the one who wronged us. It* may *heal the relationship. It* will *heal our own wounded heart.*

Consider the repercussions of not forgiving. If Joseph, the son of Jacob, had not forgiven his brothers, if he had used his high position in Egypt to "get even" with them instead, that would have been the end of the story of the children of Israel. There would be no Jewish community without this pivotal act of forgiveness. And there would be no Christian community if there had not been the central act of God's forgiveness through Christ. Forgiveness is at the very heart of who we are and why we are here as a community of faith.

When Jesus says we should forgive "seventy-seven times," he is saying we should value the wholeness of the community more than we value our own injury; and he is saying that we should, for our own sakes, choose a future free from the injuries of the past.

When we think about what Jesus said about forgiving, we are challenged to remember and to retell the bold stories which affirm that God's healing love is not just wonderful and comforting: Grace, the love of God acting in our lives, is abundant and powerful and sometimes amazing. We feel compelled to celebrate when people who were lost are found, when those who seem to have lost faith come back to life.

A good place to start is to make peace with our own past,

with our own childhood and the dysfunction of our family of origin. We may like to watch the movie *Home for the Holidays* (MGM Home Entertainment, 1995), which shows the reluctant Thanksgiving reunion of a very mixed-up family in which nothing is left unsaid, adult children feel like toddlers in the home in which they grew up, and resentments fly as wildly as attempts to "keep the peace." We say, tongue-in-cheek, that the movie reminds us how much healthier our own family is. The truth is, the family in which we were reared has a powerful influence on our identity today.

Acknowledging that, we must also avoid the generalization that there was *nothing* redemptive in our family of origin. After all, we have survived. If we do not idealize our family, we may have more understanding of the frailties in human relationships.

Even where there was terrible chaos in a family, adults have a choice about how to live now. If family gatherings are too awful, avoid them. But if there were a way that we could just "get along" for a few hours, we might begin to see family members as imperfect persons who simply did the best they knew how to do and who now regret their sins.

> *Lord, may we be forgiven for the harm we have done. May we forgive those who have harmed us. May we live in compassion. May we extend our compassion to all beings. May we never doubt your love, nor take for granted the mercy you have shown to us. Fill us with your transforming love, that we may be merciful as you are merciful. Amen*

## Step 4: Make peace with the past!

Realizing that their father was dead, Joseph's brothers said, "What if Joseph still bears a grudge against us and pays us back in full for all the wrong that we did to him?" So they approached Joseph, saying, "Your father gave this instruction before he died, 'Say to Joseph: I beg you, forgive the crime of your brothers and the wrong they did in harming you.' Now therefore please forgive the crime of the servants of the God of your father." Joseph wept when they spoke to him. Then his brothers also wept, fell down before him, and said, "We are here as your slaves." But Joseph said to them, "Do not be afraid! Am I in the place of God? Even though you intended to do harm to me, God intended it for good, in order to preserve a numerous people, as he is doing today. So have no fear; I myself will provide for you and your little ones." In this way he reassured them, speaking kindly to them.

GENESIS 50:15-21

Then Peter came and said to him, "Lord, if another member of the church sins against me, how often should I forgive? As many as seven times?" Jesus said to him, "Not seven times, but, I tell you, seventy-seven times.

MATTHEW 18:21-22

# 5

# Make Peace Within Your Household

## WEDDINGS AND FAMILIES

### Scriptural Focus ∼ Luke 2:41-52

## MESSAGE TO A BRIDE AND GROOM
## ON THEIR WEDDING DAY

Jennifer and John, you have come here today to covenant with one another in marriage. You are saying, in effect, "You are my one and only. You are my true love." As you begin this new phase of your life together, I ask you to consider these questions: How do you treat your true love? How do you speak to your true love? You have heard the old saying, "You always hurt the one you love." I think this is a reminder that the potential for hurting your true love, your spouse, is always there—because of your closeness, because of your intimacy and your special loyalty to one another. But the reverse is also true:

You have the power to affirm and strengthen one another, to protect and guide

So I ask you to think about this ahead of time. When you are tired, how will you share this with your true love? When you are angry, how will you share this with your true love? When you have a secret, how will you trust enough to speak about it to your true love, your spouse? When you suffer great pain… when you are ashamed…when you are wounded—how will you communicate these to your true love?

The Scripture readings you have chosen for your wedding reflect your intention to love and honor one another, to respect and care for one another. *"'For this reason a man shall leave his father and mother and be joined to his wife, and the two shall become one flesh'? So they are no longer two, but one flesh. Therefore what God has joined together, let no one separate"* (Matthew 19:5-6). This union of two people is not simply a merging of two separate people into one, new identity. No, you are whole and complete persons, Jennifer and John, and your union in marriage does not take away your identity. Nor does it ask you to submerge your own identity for the sake of couplehood. What this union does is to strengthen you by allowing and encouraging you to share with one another at a very deep level, to draw from the gifts and the frailties of each other, so that together you may work and love and live in a special bond—so that together you are much *more* than two persons.

Your happiness as a married couple depends upon you, Jennifer, and you, John. But you know that you are not alone. God smiles on you. Your families and friends support you. All the children of God, all the saints in heaven, and all the angels rejoice on this holy and wondrous occasion. Yes, the world will challenge you. You will face opportunities and you will face problems. Other people may cause you to wonder about your commitment. Your health may fail. You may struggle in other ways. As you grow old together, you may be asked to give more and more, to accept more and more. Let your love, which is so abundant and rich and delightful now, deepen and grow with time and understanding. Shower one another with love, the love that sustains, the love that is patient and kind…and that never fails.

You heard the Scripture: *"Love is patient; love is kind; love is not envious or boastful or arrogant or rude. It does not insist on its own way; it is not irritable or resentful; it does not rejoice in wrongdoing, but rejoices in the truth. It bears all things, believes all things, hopes all things, endures all things. Love never ends"* (1 Corinthians 13:4-8a). Remember, this treatise is about perfect love, and we are only human. We do doubt, and get tired, and impatient. We may be rude or hurtful at times. But we also have forgiveness. We have the assurance that trying to love in a perfect way is part of the growth of love. Love means saying, "I am sorry," and being willing to change a little. Love means saying, "I forgive you," and starting anew.

Jennifer and John, the Lord called you into being out of wondrous love. You have come to know and love each other, and this day, you say with all your heart, with all your being, "Jennifer, I love you truly!" "John, I love you truly!"

May the Lord shower you with every blessing, and may your love for one another grow ever stronger. Amen

⮌

Every wedding is a dream, and every word that is spoken there means more than it says, and every gesture—the clasping of hands, the giving of rings—is rich with mystery. Part of the mystery is that Christ is there as he was in Cana once, and the joy of a wedding, and maybe sometimes the tears, are a miracle that he works. But when the wedding feast was over, [Jesus] set his face toward Jerusalem and started out for the hour that had not yet come but was to come soon enough, the hour when he too was to embrace the whole earth and water it with more than his tears.

FREDERICK BUECHNER[11]

In John's Gospel, the wedding at Cana is the opening event in the ministry of Jesus. Jesus was not the host of the gathering, he was simply one of the guests. Jesus was receiving the hospitality of the family of the bride and groom. It was a personal, family setting. The miracle that Jesus performed was appropriate to the personal setting of the wedding.

It does sound like some of our families. Perhaps the food is running low and Mom is concerned, knows there will be embarrassment, and wants to help. And it seems that Mary, the mother of Jesus, noticed that the wine was running low, and she mentioned it to Jesus, who asked her what concern it was to him. And then Jesus turned water into wine, and it was the best wine. And it was in the setting of a wedding.

It's important to recall the promise and the sweetness of the wedding through the years, because peace between spouses lays the foundation for a peace-filled family life. Erma Bombeck beautifully described that journey called parenthood.

I see children as kites. You spend a lifetime trying to get them off the ground. You run with them until you're both breathless…they crash…you add a longer tail. You patch and comfort, adjust and teach—and assure them that someday they will fly. Finally they are airborne, but they need more string, and you keep letting it out. With each twist of the ball of twine, the kite becomes more distant. You know it won't be long before that beautiful creature will snap the lifeline that bound you together and soar—free and alone. Only then do you know you did your job.

ERMA BOMBECK[12]

I am well aware that there is a bittersweet quality to any focus on motherhood or fatherhood, or even family. For many, there is pride and joy and a sense of self-giving for the sake of the children, of having made the world a little happier by parental love and perseverance and devotion. For others, there is the pain of having lost a child to death or to estrangement, of having lost their own mother or father too soon. For others, there is anxiety about being needed so much by their children that they wonder how much they can give. For still others, there is the sense that soon the children will be moving on, and the fear of not being needed anymore. And for many, not being able to have children of their own is a painful reality. It's important to be respectful of mothers, fathers, grandparents, and other loving caregivers. It's important to remember and honor our own parents and grandparents and others for their response to a most challenging call.

*"His mother treasured all these things in her heart"* (Luke 2:51b). The gospel story tells us that even Jesus caused anxiety for his mother, Mary, and earthly father, Joseph. After they had spent the high holy days in Jerusalem, Jesus stayed behind. His parents thought he was with relatives and did not worry at first. When, in a panic, they realized that Jesus was not with the family, they called together friends and relatives to search for Jesus. And when they found the boy, he was seemingly oblivious to their worry.

I suppose Mary and Joseph had that same dilemma so many parents confront. Their son had challenged their wishes, not by doing something bad, but by *not* doing what was expected. He had followed his heart, confident that he was meant to study with the rabbis. Having a taste of that was very sweet—and very troubling for Mary and Joseph.

Being a parent isn't easy. It wasn't easy for Mary when her son went out to try and help the local people and they wondered what in the world he was trying to do. "Who is this guy? Isn't he just a local kid? And his father and mother— we know them; they're just ordinary people. What have they done to give the boy such *chutzpa*?"

Being a parent stretches our wildest expectations about responsibility and commitment, about love and nurturing. It means beginning at the level most intimate, and then watching and encouraging your child to become a whole and separate person. It means watching total dependence evolve into a pleasant interdependence (which lasts maybe a couple of days!), and then a gut-wrenching, heart-stopping liberation into independence.

Along the way, we learn so much. Children offer us a wisdom we are unlikely to acquire from anyone else: how to play, how to value the imagination, how to experience just being alive without having to meet everyone else's expectations or having to do anything to prove ourselves. Children teach us that we *can* take charge, that we *can* handle difficulties: staying up with the coughing child, keeping reasonably calm during that scary emergency room visit (and collapsing afterwards), laughing at our own fears, facing our humanness. And if we ever thought that perfection was something we already possessed, parenting taught us to forget it.

> *Children offer us a wisdom we are unlikely to acquire from anyone else: how to play, how to value the imagination, how to experience just being alive without having to meet everyone else's expectations or having to do anything to prove ourselves.*

My children have led me to places within myself that I had never really understood before, places that needed to grow. My children led me to experiences that have made me the person I am today. Most of all, my children taught me about interruptions: that everything in life worth doing is worth interrupting, that nothing that I want to do will get done in one sitting, and that most of what I absolutely have to do will get done in bits and pieces. I take this lesson to heart. It is a truth that keeps me centered in the midst of any challenge.

When there are challenges to a household, when the kids act up or we begin to resent or tire of the human frailties that everyone shares, it's good to remember that parents and other nurturing adults do not work alone. The Creator of the universe, the loving Christ, and the empowering Holy Spirit—

one God—works along with us, providing every grace and blessing. Peace in the home is not only possible, it is quite likely.

Celebrations of family remind us how important children really are, and how we must teach them by loving example, with a sense of humor mixed in. Sam Levinson, schoolteacher and humorist, wrote this gem many years ago, a reminder about what a gift we receive when we care for children, whether our own or another's.

> I believe that each newborn child arrives on earth with a message to deliver to [hu]mankind. Clenched in his [sic] little fist is some particle of yet unrevealed truth, some missing clue, which may solve the enigma of [our] destiny. He has a limited amount of time to fulfill his mission and he will never get a second chance—nor will we. He may be our last hope. He must be treated as top sacred.
>
> SAM LEVINSON[13]

Recall the kinds of spiritual advice adult nurturers gave to you for the living of your life: "Look on the bright side of things." "Follow your heart." "Chase your dreams." "Always tell the truth." "Do an honest day's work for an honest day's pay." "Work hard and play hard." "Family first." Reflect, too, on the advice that you would give to a young person today—to your precious son or daughter, to your dearest niece or nephew, to the teenager that you have taken under your wing, or the kid that you coach, or teach, or perhaps simply to another adult, a friend, someone whom you believe your words may help.

How many of us, when we see our children rush out into the unknown, want to protect them? We see what they do through special lenses, and we never want them to be hurt or ridiculed. We are not the only ones looking out for the child. Beside the other people who care, there is the Master of all, the Creator of all of us. And God takes whatever the child does and makes it sacred. Further, God wraps around each of us, young and old, as we play our simple little tune. And when we take those first frightening steps into the unknown— into the world of adulthood, parenthood, work, retirement— God takes us, just as we are. God works with what we have. Out of that, the Master crafts a glorious song, a masterpiece, a master work!

### Step 5: Make peace within your household!

Now every year his parents went to Jerusalem for the festival of the Passover. And when he was twelve years old, they went up as usual for the festival. When the festival was ended and they started to return, the boy Jesus stayed behind in Jerusalem, but his parents did not know it. Assuming that he was in the group of travelers, they went a day's journey. Then they started to look for him among their relatives and friends. When they did not find him, they returned to Jerusalem to search for him. After three days they found him in the temple, sitting among the teachers, listening to them and asking them questions. And all who heard him were amazed at his understanding and his answers. When his parents saw him they were astonished; and his mother said to him, "Child, why have you treated us like this? Look, your father and I have been searching for you in great anxiety." He said to them, "Why were you searching for me? Did you not know that I must be in my Father's house?" But they did not understand what he said to them. Then he went down with them and came to Nazareth, and was obedient to them. His mother treasured all these things in her heart.

LUKE 2:41-51

# 6

# Make Peace in
# Your Faith Community

## PLACE CARDS

### *Scriptural Focus* ～ *Luke 14:1,7-14*

*Said a traveler to one of the disciples,*
*"I have traveled a great distance to listen to*
*the Master,*
*but I find his words quite ordinary."*

*"Don't listen to his words.*
*Listen to his message."*

*"How does one do that?"*

*"Take hold of a sentence that he says.*
*Shake it well till all the words drop off.*
*What is left will set on fire."*

ANTHONY DE MELLO, SJ[14]

I found a snapshot of one of my aunts that had been taken the day of my parents' wedding. Aunt Annie was dressed in a dark suit, decorated with a large corsage. She wore a hat, black pumps, and white gloves. If you recall the days when hats and white gloves were absolute necessities, then you know that times have changed in our more casual world. There are, nowadays, few tea parties with a silver service, bone china, dainty little cookies, and polite conversation.

Of course, when you go to a wedding or other formal event where the tables are set beautifully, with white linen and expensive china, there *always* are place cards. As you enter the hall, you check a list to discover which table you are to sit at. You double-check the place cards at the table before you get comfortable. I suppose we hold on to that remnant of a former time—the time of white gloves and hats—to be more organized: to be sure that relatives who are not speaking to each other are seated far apart; to be sure that no one "accidentally" sits at the head table.

*"For all who exalt themselves will be humbled, and those who humble themselves will be exalted"* (Luke 14:11). Jesus tells a story about a banquet, without place cards, where nonetheless you are expected to know your place. And if you are not sure, you sit at the very end of the table, as far from the host as possible. Otherwise, Jesus warns, someone with more status may tell you to move down, and you will be very embarrassed.

We all understand this. We don't want to look foolish to others. We don't want people to think that we are arrogant or elitist. Jesus had a way of noticing those "teaching moments" that are so powerful. At a banquet, he noticed some people pushing their way up so that they could be close to the host, thinking that this association might benefit their social standing. Jesus pointed out the practical side of avoiding this: You might be embarrassed.

But if we shake the message until the words fall off, then we see that this is more than a story about manners at the table, about finding our place and staying there.

"Those who humble themselves will be exalted." Most of us are content to sit in the background. There's little danger that we would push our way to the place of honor. But what if the host of the banquet saw you sitting practically next to the door, and said to you, "Come up here. We need to talk. I have something for you to do, and it involves leadership!"?

You might respond, "Who, me? No, you must mean somebody else. I'm 'just a homemaker.'…I'm a retired person….I have small children at home. I…I…I…." And the host, who is God, says, "I know who you are. I know you completely. I know your fears and your foibles, your virtues and your challenges. But I love you and I want you to do something special for me. So, come up higher."

Humility means *knowing* who we are and *being* who we are—no more, no less. It is being true to ourselves and true to God, who created us. If we are puffed up with arrogance, something will come along to remind us that false pride is not honest.

Most of us are not puffed up with arrogance. In fact, we are more likely at the other end of the curve. We think less of ourselves than we should. We may apologize too much. We may even say, "I'm not good enough." This is not humility. You are a precious child of God!

God created us perfectly, in God's own image. And when we serve others, we are exalted. When we choose to remain in the background instead of always in the seat of honor, God loves that. And when we know that we must be in the center, in a position of prominence, God loves that too. Even in the limelight, we are grounded in the knowledge that we are all brothers and sisters and that no one person is more worthy of God's love than any other.

We all have gifts, God-given gifts. Using our gifts may mean doing a little volunteer work at church. Remembering our spiritual center while we are at work is using the gift of love in the workplace. Spending time with grandchildren is using our love of family to share our gifts with little ones, the ones whom Jesus said were the special treasures of our life. Paul wrote, "*Do you not know that you are God's temple and that God's Spirit dwells in you?*" (1 Corinthians 3:16). You are the temple of God and the Spirit of God dwells in you…all the time: when you are sleeping, when you are washing dishes, when you are car-pooling the children to Little League.

> *You are the temple of God and the Spirit of God dwells in you…all the time: when you are sleeping, when you are washing dishes, when you are car-pooling the children to Little League.*

Perhaps God is calling you, and me, to expand our notion of what we can do. Jesus, our brother, sometimes caused people to feel uncomfortable. That is why some who heard him rejected his message, and others took a leap of faith and did things they never imagined to be possible. "If you want peace, work for justice" (Pope Paul VI).[15]

The gospel story is also about the gathering itself. This gathering is a sacred coming together of a faith community.

It's a living definition of community. Whom do we invite? Do we invite the richest people we know, so that when we need money we have someone to lean on? Do we invite the people with prestige—the superintendent of schools, or the congressional representative—so that they will remember us when we have trouble with education or politics? Do we stop writing invitations when we come to the people who can't afford to dress up and who will not be able to reciprocate with their own party next month? Do we leave out poor people, homeless people, persons with chronic illness, men, women, and children who are in need? Or do we invite and welcome everyone? Are we ready for the repercussions of unity?

Our gracious Creator, in wisdom and love, has invited us to the wedding feast by gifting us with community. Yet, we sometimes cling a little too tightly to our invitation, to our own way of thinking. We sometimes set limits for others at the table. Throughout history, we have imposed false limitations on that gift called the community of the people of God. That is changing.

The German philosopher Schopenhauer, in a pessimistic observation, compared the human race to a bunch of porcupines huddling together on a cold winter's night. He said:

> The colder it gets outside, the more we huddle together for warmth; but the closer we get to one another, the more we hurt one another with our sharp quills. And in the lonely night of earth's winter eventually we begin to drift apart and wander out on our own and freeze to death in our loneliness.

ARTHUR SCHOPENHAUER[16]

Isn't that depressing? A contemporary writer has added a positive note: "Christ has given us an alternative—to forgive each other for the pokes we receive. That allows us to stay together and stay warm" (Edward Himilton).[17]

And the famous Rev. Moody writes: "There are two ways of being united—one is by being frozen together, and the other is by being melted together. What Christians need is to be united in brotherly love, and then they may expect to have power."[18] Perhaps a little more warmth would help.

~

In preparing to teach a course in Contemporary World Religions, I noticed that virtually every faith tradition has some version of what we call "The Golden Rule," i.e., *Do unto others as you would have them do unto you.* In fact, I found a jigsaw puzzle, a replica of a Norman Rockwell classic, entitled "The Golden Rule." And as I worked on the puzzle, I reflected on the picture—a collage of faces of people of every race and creed, women, men, children, babies, all together. It's a powerful view of what community looks like: not a sameness that means that everyone looks alike, thinks alike, believes alike. No, community is a group of persons who have a common core, or center, a belief in God—known by a variety of names—and a commitment to love God, neighbor, and self.

Why is community so essential? You and I are here, not because of a random happening. God, who works in our lives even when we are not really paying attention, has brought us to this time and place for a purpose. We may not fully understand the reason, but we can speculate.

Could it be that God calls us here, now, so that we can

use our gifts in community and so that we can receive what we need in community? In a perfect world, everyone's needs and gifts would match up perfectly. Our task, as people of God here and now, is to identify and use our precious gifts to help others, and to return to God a part of what has been given to us. "For all who exalt themselves will be humbled, and those who humble themselves will be exalted." When you take the message and shake off all the words, what do you hear? What do you feel? Does it set your heart on fire? Does it warm you just a little?

> *"For all who exalt themselves will be humbled, and those who humble themselves will be exalted." When you take the message and shake off all the words, what do you hear? What do you feel? Does it set your heart on fire? Does it warm you just a little?*

Finally, here is a challenge, expressed so beautifully by a contemporary writer who calls herself Oriah Mountain Dreamer. Consider it carefully and prayerfully, and see if it speaks to you.

> *It doesn't interest me what you do for a living.*
> *I want to know what you ache for and if you*
> *dare to dream of meeting your heart's longing.*
> *It doesn't interest me how old you are.*
> *I want to know if you will risk looking like a fool*
> *for love, for your dream, for the adventure of*
> *being alive.*
> *It doesn't interest me what planets are squaring your*
> *moon.*

*I want to know if you have touched the center of
        your own sorrow, if you have been opened
        by life's betrayals, or have become shriveled
        and closed from fear of further pain.*

*I want to know if you can sit with pain, mine or
        your own, without moving to hide it or fade
        it or fix it.*

*I want to know if you can be with joy, mine or
        your own;*

*If you can dance with wildness and let the
        ecstasy fill you to the tips of your fingers and
        toes, without cautioning us to be careful, to
        be realistic, to remember the limitations of
        being human.*

*It doesn't interest me if the story you are telling me is
        true.*

*I want to know if you can disappoint another to
        be true to yourself.*

*If you can bear the accusation of betrayal and
        not betray your own soul.*

*If you can be faithful and therefore trustworthy.*

*I want to know if you can see beauty even when
        it is not pretty every day.*

*And if you can source your own life from its
        presence.*

*I want to know if you can live with failure, yours
        and mine, and still stand on the edge of the
        lake and shout to the silver of the full moon,
        "Yes."*

*It doesn't interest me to know where you live or how
        much money you have.*

*I want to know if you can get up after a night of*
*grief and despair, weary and bruised to the*
*bone, and do what needs to be done to feed*
*the children.*
*It doesn't interest me who you know or how you*
*came to be here.*
*I want to know if you will stand in the center of*
*the fire with me and not shrink back.*
*It doesn't interest me where or what or with whom*
*you have studied.*
*I want to know what sustains you from the*
*inside when all else falls away.*
*I want to know if you can be alone with yourself,*
*and if you truly like the company you keep in*
*the empty moments.*

ORIAH MOUNTAIN DREAMER[19]

## Step 6: Make peace in your faith community!

On one occasion when Jesus was going to the house of a leader of the Pharisees to eat a meal on the sabbath, they were watching him closely.

When he noticed how the guests chose the places of honor, he told them a parable. "When you are invited by someone to a wedding banquet, do not sit down at the place of honor, in case someone more distinguished than you has been invited by your host; and the host who invited both of you may come and say to you, 'Give this person your place,' and then in disgrace you would start to take the lowest place. But when you are invited, go and sit down at the lowest place, so that when your host comes, he may say to you, 'Friend, move up higher'; then you will be honored in the presence of all who sit at the table with you. For all who exalt themselves will be humbled, and those who humble themselves will be exalted."

He said also to the one who had invited him, "When you give a luncheon or a dinner, do not invite your friends or your brothers or your relatives or rich neighbors, in case they may invite you in return, and you would be repaid. But when you give a banquet, invite the poor, the crippled, the lame, and the blind. And you will be blessed, because they cannot repay you, for you will be repaid at the resurrection of the righteous."

LUKE 14:1,7-14

# 7

# Respond When Peace Is Threatened

## STORM AT SEA

*Scriptural Focus* ～ *Luke 8:22-25*

There is a great deal of tension in our world, a sense of not being as safe as we once believed we were. This tension is manifesting itself as depression, as anxiety, and confusion. In an environment that includes negativity, how do we keep calm, keep focused on our work, our goals, our challenges, without being drawn into the storm?

Jesus had a way of bringing calm even in the most tense situations, and he tells us that we, here and now, can expect the same from him. I love the ocean, and yet I am afraid of the ocean. In the angry waves on a stormy day, I see what power is, and how ocean floods destroy the beaches and the homes along the edges of the land. I am fascinated by storms. I have seen many in my life, and I'm amazed at how the sun comes up the morning after, as if nothing has happened. I have been afraid in the middle of a storm, whether those squalls that seem to rise up out of nowhere in the summer or the biting chill of a "nor'easter" in winter. And when I'm very afraid, I find myself praying that we will all be safe.

A fierce storm. Jesus coming to the rescue. Then, a great calm. This story of Jesus in the boat with his disciples has all the elements of high drama: darkness, wind, water, flooding. And we see all the related emotions: fear, confusion, despair. And we witness a miracle: Jesus calms the storm, calms the sea, and that's that.

But as usual, this is more than a simple narrative. There is something in here for you and me. There was nothing unusual about going out at night in the boat. Several of the apostles were fishermen, and they worked nights. There was nothing unusual about stormy seas; these summer squalls were not unusual. But somehow, even the weathered fishermen sensed something sinister about this particular storm. They began to be afraid, that kind of fear that starts from the edges of the heart and causes a deep chill or a high anxiety. They actually feared that the boat would capsize and they would die!

They looked over at Jesus and saw that he was sleeping… sleeping…in spite of their terror! In their emotion, they were angry with Jesus for not noticing, for not understanding their fear. They yelled at him, "Don't you know that we are about to die? And there you are, oblivious to our pain!"

Then Jesus calmly got up and ended the crisis… "and there was a calm." And when the storm was over and the waves were calm, no one was afraid of the storm anymore. Now they were afraid of Jesus! What kind of man was this who could stop the storms, who could save us even when we knew we were going to die?

I like this miracle story. I am impressed when, Poof!, with a wave of the hand, a problem is solved and life goes on. But that doesn't happen often with me, nor does it with you, I would guess. It's comforting to hear that Jesus saved his friends with a word. It's assuring to know that Jesus has the power to literally turn our lives right-side-up again when we face calamities in our lives. Christ did not come to eliminate suffering, or to explain it, but to fill it with his presence.

Reading between the lines of the gospel story, we know that the fishermen did not simply stand there in panic when the crisis was upon them. We can be sure that they did everything in their power, used all the resources of their own strength and experience, before concluding that they were not going to get through this alone. And they show us that sometimes our own efforts are just not enough.

> Every problem has in it the seeds of its own solution….[W]hen the Lord wants to give you [an important teaching], He doesn't wrap it in a sophisticated package and hand it to you on a silver platter….[God] buries it at the heart of a big, tough problem. How He must watch with delight when you've got what it takes to break that problem apart and find at its heart what the Bible calls, "the pearl of great price." Everybody I've ever known who succeeded in a big way in life has done so by breaking problems apart and finding the value that was there.
>
> NORMAN VINCENT PEALE[20]

On the night when Jesus calmed the storm, he commented, with his usual candor, that the followers had no need to panic; they had their faith. But be careful not to assume that having faith means having answers. Having faith means we trust that God is in control, but we may still be afraid. Having faith doesn't mean that we will be strong at every moment of our lives, or that no harm will ever befall us.

> *Having faith doesn't mean that we will be strong at every moment of our lives, or that no harm will ever befall us.*

We have to be careful about spreading what can sound like a platitude—that our faith will see us through. Well, of course it will. But God gives us faith, and still we sometimes feel alone. Sometimes we feel that God is not around at all, or is being unnecessarily silent. And sometimes the storms or difficulties in our life last a long time.

Some miracles are quick and some miracles take a long time. In our biblical narratives about Jesus, we hear about the quick miracles; we may have to look pretty hard to see the ones that take a long time. But Jesus is working in our lives, and much of his working is involved in *process*, in the growth and healing that take time. Working for peace, especially when peace is threatened, is a process of healing. What doesn't work?

For centuries now we've tried everything else; the power of wealth, of mighty armies and navies, machinations of diplomats. All have failed. Before it's too late, and time is running out, let us turn from trust in the chain reactions of exploding atoms to faith in the chain reaction of God's love. Love—love of God and fellow men [sic]. That is God's formula for peace. Peace on earth to [people] of good will.

RICHARD CARDINAL CUSHING[21]

If we were knocked to the ground by a bolt of light, as Saint Paul was, or if we were instantly cured of a chronic illness, then we might be able to dramatically change our life. Mostly, though, God is working in us, growing us, forming us slowly—and it takes a lifetime to be whole or holy. Sometimes our lives turn in ways that are mysterious, like a difficult path in deep snow.

You may have seen the cartoon about the person who's feeling inadequate, with the caption, "God isn't finished with me yet." We may sometimes wonder why our Lord seems to be so hard to grasp, not listening, or simply ignoring us. This does not mean that God has abandoned us. Neither does it mean that we have little faith. The question is how to deal with this sense of being vulnerable, or helpless, or even defensive. What helps us when we are afraid or hurt or lonely?

We know that "hanging on" helps. We know admitting that we are dealing with a crisis, and working to figure out our feelings and thoughts, helps. We know that telling our story to someone who can help us is useful when times are tough. If we consider how the followers of Jesus dealt with him after his death and Resurrection, when they had to carry on without his physical presence, we can certainly imagine that they reached back into their memories for times when Jesus was there to heal them, to take away their fears, to stop the winds and the waters, to calm the storm.

Remembering Jesus certainly doesn't erase whatever we struggle with. But remembering Jesus may very well help us, whether the sea is angry or calm, whether the skies are dark gray or bright blue. I do think that when we share with others an experience such as that scene with the apostles, we see more clearly than usual how we are all connected, how we are all brothers and sisters, children of the one God. When someone else suffers, we suffer, too. When someone else rejoices in a healing experience, we rejoice with them. And when healing comes to a community, we can see God at work through the faith of God's people.

Healing involves a process in which the individual or the community removes obstacles to understanding and becomes receptive to God's healing power. The person or body of persons comes to believe and know that God loves them—just as they are. The miracle stories in the Bible remind us that only God, the divine Physician, can make us whole and holy.

There is a blind man who trusts that Jesus can give him back his sight. He takes the bold step of approaching Jesus, whom he only knows by reputation, so that Jesus might heal him. And how does Jesus respond? Jesus takes him for a walk. Slowly, the man begins to see, first a shadowy kind of vision, then very, very clearly. Jesus walks with him, helping him to see more clearly. The journey of a soul.

I like this account because it reminds me that healing may take time. It reminds me that Christ's Spirit walks with me, helps me to see more clearly, accompanies me on the journey, the long and winding road of my life. Some miracles are immediate, once and for all; some take time, even a lifetime. Recently, research has been shown that people who are ill and who are prayed for really get better faster than those who are not prayed for. Isn't it wonderful when research "proves" something that we have believed all along?

"After centuries of slow progress toward rational explanations of the physical world, even scientists can at last begin to appreciate that…faith, belief, and imagination can actually unlock the mysteries of healing" (Joan Borysenko).[22] The message is clear. We need to be bold in our asking and active in our healing process. Dr. Bernie Siegel, the New Haven surgeon who shifted his focus from cutting out the cancer to helping his patients heal, recommends that we all become "difficult" patients; that is, we question every option, speak up for ourselves, take control of our lives, and surround ourselves with allies who will fight for the truth.

Jesus responded to boldness, to someone coming to him and having the courage to ask for what he needed, to ask for healing. Jesus responded to the outcast, entering into the crowd to have contact with him. People wanted simply to be healed, and they were totally healed.

Sometimes we are hesitant to ask boldly, because we think it's not humble. Jesus *never* said we should think of ourselves as unworthy. No, he said we are all children of God, and God wants the children to come to him, just as parents want and expect their children to come to them for help. Humility means recognizing God's grace and love and power within us and around us.

Sometimes we hesitate to pray for what we need because we feel unworthy of healing. Jesus invited his followers then, and he invites us here today, to ask for *anything* in prayer. It will be granted, according to the will of the Father.

↪

There are people who believe that illness and adversity are sent by God as a "test" or as a "lesson." We may learn something from our troubles or we may not, and if we do, it may take a long, long time. Life is not a test. Bad things do not happen to us to test us. Look at such a theology logically: God sends you an illness as a test. How are the results evaluated? How do you get a good grade? If you cry and moan because you are hurting, does that mean that you failed the test? On the other hand, if you are stoic and silent, does that mean that you passed this test and you can move on to more difficult ones? When your time on this physical plane is complete, do you just test out? And then what? No more tests? Newer and more exciting tests? See what I mean?

I was in North Dakota for several years, including the winter of 1996-1997. That season, we were socked with fifteen blizzards, and then—when we wondered how it could get any worse—there were awful floods, as the Red River (which flows to the north) spilled over its banks with the run-off from too much snow melting too fast and too much water trying to push through passages blocked by trees and rocks.

People lost their homes. That nice man from FEMA, whom you see on TV, came up, and soon many workers came to help. The President and Vice-President of the United States came to show their concern. The Red Cross trained church leaders in ways to help people deal with the aftermath, because the trauma of the winter brought many of us, mentally and emotionally, back to places we thought we had passed, to earlier times in our lives when we had felt helpless and isolated.

Trailers were set up for families who had no place to call

home, but the trailers had no heat, and by the following winter homes were still not rebuilt. The land was devastated; it was too wet for farmers to plant, and some lost everything. Some older folks were so filled with compassion and grief for all those who suffered that they themselves got sick. Several of our people died, from pneumonia, clinically, but really, from sadness.

I heard many people say that the winter of 1996-1997 was a "test" from God as a punishment for sin. And this is not unsophisticated country wisdom. We all seek the reasons for why terrible things happen—the "black box" that will explain it all. When something absolutely awful happens, we want a rational explanation. Often, it's easier to blame ourselves, especially if we were trained, way back when, to think that God and guilt and shame go together.

Life is not about failing tests, or working harder and harder to "please" a demanding "Boss." Life is about living through the moments, doing what we can, given our particular gifts, to love God and to love one another, no matter what.

Healing of persons and healing of nations are, I believe, connected. What Joel Goldsmith wrote in 1959 is still true today:

> The world is not in need of a new religion, nor is the world in need of a new philosophy: What the world needs is healing and regeneration. The world needs people who, through devotion to God, are so filled with the Spirit that they can be the instruments through which healing takes place, because healing is important to everybody.
>
> JOEL GOLDSMITH[23]

People used to say, "Into each life a little rain must fall." For some of us, it seems that the rain is torrential, the winds are hurricane force, the skies are thick with angry clouds, the roof has holes in it and there is no one around with a bucket, the wetness gets into our joints, and we are hurting. It is important to remember that the One who made the rain, who configured the heavens, and who loves us greatly, will send a rainbow. And in the meantime, that same Creator God holds an umbrella over our lives and keeps us safe until the sun shines again.

## Step 7: Respond when peace is threatened!

One day he got into a boat with his disciples, and he said to them, "Let us go across to the other side of the lake." So they put out, and while they were sailing he fell asleep. A windstorm swept down on the lake, and the boat was filling with water, and they were in danger. They went to him and woke him up, shouting, "Master, Master, we are perishing!" And he woke up and rebuked the wind and the raging waves; they ceased, and there was a calm. He said to them, "Where is your faith?" They were afraid and amazed, and said to one another, "Who then is this, that he commands even the winds and the water, and they obey him?"

LUKE 8:22-25

# 8

# Make Peace in Your Corner of the World

## THE CHALLENGE OF DIVERSITY

*Scriptural Focus* ～ *Philippians 4:4-7*

It all started with a letter to Ann Landers!

Dear Ann Landers:

The original source is unknown, and I'm not sure if the information is still current, but the message is certainly thought-provoking. It's called a "Summary of the World Facts":

If we could shrink the Earth's population to a village of precisely 100 people...with all existing human ratios remaining the same, it would look like this:

There would be 57 Asians, 21 Europeans, 14 from the Western Hemisphere (North and South) and 8 Africans.

51 would be female; 49 male.

70 would be nonwhite; 30 white.

70 would be non-Christian; 30 Christian.

50 percent of the entire world's wealth would be in the hands of only 6 people, and all 6 would be citizens of the United States.

80 would live in substandard housing.

70 would be unable to read.

50 would suffer from malnutrition.

1 would be near death, 1 would be near birth.

Only 1 would have a college education.

No one would own a computer!![24]

If we consider our world from a compressed perspective, what do we see? We need to understand that our own perspective may be limited in some ways, our own view of the world may be too small. Consider this piece from the newspaper:

With the crash landing of Pathfinder on the surface of Mars, we go in search of answers to Earth's history. Although it was once much like our own watery blue marble in space, no one knows what happened to Mars and its atmosphere, its lakes and rivers. As the rover Sojourner probes its way across the Martian surface, researchers hope they can collect clues to how life got started and how our planet might evolve in the future.[25]

There was a time, of course, when everyone thought Earth to be the center of the universe. Now we are reminded that our planet Earth is just one of many. And our nearest neighbor, Mars, is looking very interesting. Is our world view too small? We are presented with challenges to ponder and attempts to awaken us to a world that is larger than our own little corner. We are presented with an opportunity to adopt a wider world view of our lives as Christians.

When Jesus went to the synagogue to do what he was called to do, to speak out in a new voice what God had made plain to him, he was confronted with a familiar dilemma. He was a local man. Everyone knew his family. Everyone had known him as a child and as a young man, and basically thought they really knew all about him. Then Jesus, who was the son of a woodworker, surprised everyone by challenging his own people to wake up from their daily lethargic existence and look at the larger picture. He asked them to remember who they were: the people of God, with a heritage as children of the Creator and as stewards of God's gifts, and with a clearly articulated call to holiness! He challenged them to expand their world view.

Jesus reminded the people of what most had forgotten: that being a person of God means having respect for God and respect for neighbor. In their rejection of Jesus, the people showed that they were guilty of the small-mindedness that says: "Don't make us uncomfortable. We know how to live. Who are you, anyway?"

What could people have done to really hear Jesus? They could have come in a spirit of prayer. They could have been open to God speaking to them through someone who seemed very ordinary to them. They could have tried to listen to him.

They could have tried to understand him, instead of reject-ing him. They could have been open to him. They could have considered what their spiritual life was like and how Jesus challenged them to be transformed. They could have looked at the larger picture and broken out of their limited view of the world. They could have been humble. They could have been bold enough to change their lives in response to Jesus.

But most rejected him.

How would you or I react to Jesus in our place of wor-ship, standing at the pulpit and challenging us to look at the bigger picture, that is, to look at what God expects of us? How would we react to Jesus, who came to give sight to the blind and to heal the sick, and who confronted the compla-cent until they felt very uncomfortable?

I believe that we are called to look around in our little corner of the world and find ways to bring healing and for-giveness to others. We are called to live in a way that demon-strates our conviction that God loves us and forgives us, and that we are expected to do the same for others. May God guide us to those places where we are needed and into the hearts of those who seek to know the Lord.

How do we go about listening to voices that seem differ-ent from our own? How do we respond to the challenge of Jesus? How do we get beyond our limited viewpoint, in or-der to understand our role in a world that is complex and diverse and richly beautiful?

*How do we get beyond our limited viewpoint, in order to understand our role in a world that is complex and diverse and richly beautiful?*

Discomfort is part of our lot as Christians, as people of God in this world, in this universe. Christians are called to "comfort the afflicted and to afflict the comfortable." We live in an expanding world, and yet, we may find comfort in staying within the artificial borders we draw around ourselves. It's safer that way; it's not so scary—until perhaps one day we look around and realize that we have not lived fully.

Expanding our world view involves restructuring our little corner of the world. For us, this involves making our local church community more responsive to the radical message of Jesus, to the words and actions of Jesus which caused his neighbors to wonder: "Where did he get this knowledge? Isn't he just one of us?" As someone once asked: If you resist hearing what you disagree with, how will you ever understand what you do believe? The things most worth listening to are precisely those that challenge your mind.

What we can do is muster the courage to show compassion for others, *all* others—those within our community and those in the rest of the world. We can have the courage to listen to and really hear views that are patently different from our own, and even to worship our God with persons we perceive as "other." In order to love God, we need to love our sisters and brothers. In this ever-expanding world, where we are more and more aware of the vastness of God and the whole created order, we might ask ourselves, "Is my world too small?"

### Step 8: Make peace in your corner of the world!

Rejoice in the Lord always; again I will say, Rejoice. Let your gentleness be known to everyone. The Lord is near. Do not worry about anything, but in everything by prayer and supplication with thanksgiving let your requests be made known to God. And the peace of God, which surpasses all understanding, will guard your hearts and your minds in Christ Jesus.

PHILIPPIANS 4:4-7

# 9

# Make Peace in Your Homeland

## HE'S MY BROTHER

*Scriptural Focus* ~ *Matthew 11:16-19,25-30*

*The road is long*
*With many a winding turn*
*That leads us to who knows where*
*Who knows when*
*But I'm strong*
*Strong enough to carry him*
*He ain't heavy, he's my brother*

*So on we go*
*His welfare is my concern*
*No burden is he to bear*
*We'll get there*
*For I know*
*He would not encumber me*
*He ain't heavy, he's my brother*

*If I'm laden at all*
*I'm leaning with sadness*
*That everyone's heart*
*Isn't filled with the gladness*
*Of love for one another*

*It's a long, long road*
*From which there is no return*
*While we're on the way to there*
*Why not share*
*And the load*
*Doesn't weigh me down at all*
*He ain't heavy, he's my brother*

*He's my brother*
*He ain't heavy, he's my brother…*[26]

Jesus said, "Come to me, all you that are weary and are carrying heavy burdens, and I will give you rest. Take my yoke upon you, and learn from me; for I am gentle and humble in heart, and you will find rest for your souls. For my yoke is easy, and my burden is light."

MATTHEW 11:28-30

How can this be? How could the yoke Jesus speaks about ever be easy, and how could a yoke possibly be associated with rest for our souls? How can we take up another burden and rest easy at the same time? *What does it mean to share a yoke?* A man who grew up on a farm explains.

When I was a boy at home, I used to drive the oxen. The yoke was never made to balance, as many think. The yokes were always made heavier on one side than the other. Then we would put a weak bullock in alongside a strong bullock; the light end would come on the weak ox, the heavier end on the stronger one. That's why the yoke is easy and the burden is light, because the Lord's yoke is made after the same pattern, and the heavy end is upon his shoulder.

STEVE ELY[27]

So, friend, when we take upon us the yoke of Jesus, we can be assured that he carries whatever we cannot bear. Jesus is our brother, our bigger and stronger brother, and we are not heavy in his care. Love is the equalizer that makes each of us, no matter how relatively weak or strong, able to help carry the burden of someone else.

Our brother or sister in Christ, someone we love, is never too heavy for us. On our patriotic holidays, such as July 4th, we celebrate our independence as citizens of these United States of America. We consider how we can express our compassion and freedom with our brothers and sisters here and throughout the world because *We hold these truths to be self-evident: that all men are created equal, that they are endowed by their creator with certain unalienable rights, that among these are life, liberty, and the pursuit of happiness* (The Declaration of Independence July 4, 1776).

The people who tried to put into words our vision as Americans wrote our national declaration of independence. They articulated both our responsibilities and our rights. They assumed that all persons are equal, and that all are children of God, with the birthright and the inheritance of the people of God. Within the lines, we continue to understand more fully that our individual freedom, our own pursuit of happiness, needs to take into account our communal rights and freedoms. We are not alone. We are part of a much greater totality, and we cannot put our own agenda before that of others.

> No man is an island, entire of itself; every man is a piece of the continent, a part of the main. Any man's death diminishes me, because I am involved in mankind, and therefore never tend to know for whom the bell tolls; it tolls for thee.

JOHN DONNE[28]

We know that whenever the freedom of another person is deadened, we are less alive, whereas when the freedom of another person is rejuvenated, we are more alive. We revel in flowing flags, brass bands, firecrackers and skyrockets, patriotic hymns, and prayers for peace.

We are not alone. And being free means helping to carry the burdens of others, so that their yoke is sweeter and their burden is a little lighter. The welfare of our brothers and sisters is something we have to care about.

As we celebrate this most extroverted holiday, our country's independence, perhaps we should take time to go to a quiet place and balance our thankfulness for our independence with an appreciation of our interdependence. As the diverse colonies and the individual patriots depended upon each other and acted in accord in order to achieve freedom, so must we depend on one another to protect our freedoms, and to extend them to those who have not yet enjoyed liberty.

As John Donne suggested, we are not alone, we are each "a part of the main." We are each a part of a community, a country, an ecosystem, a cosmos. What we do has repercussions for the whole. We are dependent on the whole for our moment to moment existence. We are many and yet we are one.

> *What we do has repercussions for the whole. We are dependent on the whole for our moment to moment existence. We are many and yet we are one.*

Let us give thanks for the freedoms we enjoy. As we breathe in, may we feel the joy of independence. As we breathe out, may we feel the power of interdependence. Feeling the power of interdependence, we give up false divisions. Giving up false divisions, we feel a part of a whole. We experience peace, we feel compassion for all beings, we find refuge in the great union of life. We remember that we are here to share one another's burdens, and when we do that, each of us is lifted a little higher.

This is particularly important in view of the larger stresses that we are all aware of and that we must deal with. Our society is faced with wars and violence and other problems, near and far. This is not the time to replace trust with fear. We may be troubled by the negative events that are spotlighted in our culture. Still, we know that God is good, God is in control, and we are all God's children. There is more hope, more light, more peace, than we could possibly imagine. And there is wonderful potential for people who focus on peace, who really think peace and live peace, and are willing to share their blessings and their challenges.

> The brilliance of mind, the beauty in our hearts, and the [presence of] divinity of our spirits has equipped us with everything we need to turn the course of civilization around in a more positive direction. [What we need to do first is to adjust our values and attitudes.]....If we get our minds and hearts aligned, everything else will fall into place.
>
> KEN KALB[29]

In other words, as the song says, "Let there be peace on earth, and let it begin with me."

## FUNDAMENTAL ATTITUDINAL ADJUSTMENTS

1. We must acknowledge our problems fully.
2. We must think in terms of We, instead of just Me.
3. Humanity must consider itself a global family, working and playing in unity in our diversity and harmony in our variety.
4. Business leaders and corporations must open their hearts and practice compassionate capitalism, where the prime directive of increasing wealth equally considers enhancing the quality of life and maintaining our delicate and vital balances.
5. We must elect and empower enlightened spiritual leaders who use their...pulpit and our vast resources to invigorate inspirational programs to meet and beat our challenges.

6. Our collective will, imagination, and passion must be ignited so we are inspired to spring into action.
7. We must live with a golden rule mentality where we treat others and Mother [Earth] as we would like to be treated ourselves.
8. We must all dig a little deeper and shine a little brighter.[30]

If we do this right, our only regret will be that we didn't start sooner and that we have still farther to go before everyone is singing the same tune.

～

President Abraham Lincoln often visited hospitals to talk with wounded soldiers during the Civil War. Once, doctors pointed out a young soldier who was near death and Lincoln went over to his bedside.

"Is there anything I can do for you?" asked the President.

The soldier obviously didn't recognize Lincoln, and with some effort he was able to whisper, "Would you please write a letter to my mother?"

A pen and paper were provided and the President carefully began to write down what the young man was able to say:

"My dearest mother, I was badly hurt while doing my duty. I'm afraid I'm not going to recover. Don't grieve too much for me, please. Kiss Mary and John for me. May God bless you and father."

The soldier was too weak to continue, so Lincoln signed the letter for him and added, "Written for your son by Abraham Lincoln."

The young man asked to see the note and was astonished when he discovered who had written it. "Are you really the president?" he asked.

"Yes, I am," Lincoln replied quietly. Then he asked if there was anything else he could do.

"Would you please hold my hand?" the soldier asked. "It will help to see me through to the end." In the hushed room, the tall gaunt President took the boy's hand in his and spoke warm words of encouragement until death came.[31]

I like this story because it reminds me that we are all equal. Everyone, no matter what his or her stature, can give a kindness and receive a kindness.

### Step 9: Make peace in your homeland!

> But to what will I compare this generation? It is like children sitting in the marketplaces and calling to one another,
> "We played the flute for you, and you did not dance; we wailed, and you did not mourn."
> For John came neither eating nor drinking, and they say, "He has a demon"; the Son of Man came eating and drinking, and they say, "Look, a glutton and a drunkard, a friend of tax collectors and sinners!" Yet wisdom is vindicated by her deeds.

MATTHEW 11:16-19

I thank you, Father, Lord of heaven and earth, because you have hidden these things from the wise and the intelligent and have revealed them to infants; yes, Father, for such was your gracious will. All things have been handed over to me by my Father; and no one knows the Son except the Father, and no one knows the Father except the Son and anyone to whom the Son chooses to reveal him.

Come to me, all you that are weary and are carrying heavy burdens, and I will give you rest. Take my yoke upon you, and learn from me; for I am gentle and humble in heart, and you will find rest for your souls. For my yoke is easy, and my burden is light.

MATTHEW 11:25-30

# 10

# Make Peace in the World

*Scriptural Focus* ∽ *Revelation 21:1-6a*

A little boy listened carefully as his missionary teacher explained why it is that Christians give presents to each other on Christmas Day. "The gift is an expression of our joy over the birth of Jesus and our friendship for each other," she said. When Christmas Day came, the boy brought the teacher a sea shell of lustrous beauty.

"Where did you ever find such a beautiful shell?" the teacher asked. The youth told her that there was only one spot where such extraordinary shells could be found—a certain bay several miles away.

"Why...why, it's gorgeous," said the teacher. "But you shouldn't have gone all that way to get a gift for me."

His eyes brightening, the boy answered, "Long walk part of gift."

JAMES S. HEWETT[32]

Several years ago, on December 31, 1999, we all received a gift. All of the world shared a moment together. The century changed and the whole world waited together to see what would happen. Nobody knew for sure if our computer dependent society would face disruption, and we watched to see what would occur as the world turned. Midnight struck in each time zone from the islands of the Pacific to Asia, Europe and Africa, and finally the Americas. We watched on TV through twenty-four time zones to see if any of the often-predicted problems would bring disaster. As we watched, we became more aware of the nature of this planet, this humanity, this global culture we've grown. The world as we know it did not end, as some had predicted it would, but maybe it changed a little.

I couldn't help but think about how all these nations—so different, so diverse—all cooperated so that the broadcast was coordinated perfectly. And I have kept thinking about this. If we can all work together on one fine day for a few hours in perfect harmony, then there must be a potential for even greater things. Why not worldwide peace, even for a day? Why not love and forgiveness, even for a day? Why not celebrate our unity as children of God and not concentrate on what we have allowed to separate us, even for a day? I was awed by the possibilities before us.

> *Why not worldwide peace, even for a day? Why not love and forgiveness, even for a day? Why not celebrate our unity as children of God and not concentrate on what we have allowed to separate us, even for a day?*

I felt connected, as I never have before, to real people around the earth. For almost everybody alive today, the twentieth century has been the only century we've experienced. It has been a time of amazing change. Wonderful things have developed in the past one hundred years. And yet it has been a century of incredible destruction and horror as well.

Now we have the opportunity to make a new start. Historians will look at the years 1900 through 1999 as a unit, and the year 2000 will be a milestone. It is a page turned, a new chapter started. It is a psychological opportunity to begin anew to create a better world. We have learned much about our world and about what it takes to develop healthy human beings. Let's put it into practice.

We all want to change the world. Most of us want to change something about ourselves too. We look around, or we look inside, and we see much that is unsatisfactory. Sometimes things look so bad that we feel like giving up. When we talk with others these days about the state of the world, we often are met with a sense of hopelessness. Some things look so bad we can't see how they might get better.

During the months that the countdown to the year 2000 took place, we heard a lot of frightening predictions. If we allow dire predictions to penetrate our hearts, we can become hopeless and depressed. Then we can become paralyzed, and do nothing. It is vital to remember this: As a people, as the children of God, we may not be able to solve all our problems, but we can influence our surroundings. We can even change the world!

There was a man who had a motto: Park up front. He noticed that most people anticipate the lack of a parking spot close to the entry to an event, so they take the first spot they see in the back of the lot. He practiced visualizing a parking place near the entrance, and he always got it. He said, "You just set your intention to the better things, and you usually receive what is good."

We all know that when we expect the worst, we usually get it. My first reaction to this was, "Yeah, sure!" But in thinking about my own expectations about life, when I foresee what is good and strong and healthy, that's what I receive most often. When I get really anxious and expect the worst, I often get the worst.

I do believe that once we become open to the possibility of "little miracles," they seem to happen more frequently. People show up at just the right time, when we need them. I remember a day when I was feeling really discouraged, and I didn't know how to handle it. The telephone rang, and it was an old friend who was able to help me. I open my daily devotional and the message is exactly what I need to read, even though I know that the collection was put together many months ago, by strangers. I meet someone through seemingly accidental circumstances, and that person brings amazing meaning to a part of my life.

I'm not saying that I always get my way. Sometimes what I want, or think is good for me, is just not in the game plan. But I am more likely to see wonderful happenings if I am attentive to them.

At Christmastide, we are reminded very powerfully of the love of God in sending Jesus of Nazareth to this Earth. We see, in the humble stable, a loving family. We can see that, though Jesus met a great deal of opposition in his ministry, he was faithful to his call to bring to humanity a consciousness of its individual and collective responsibility: to love one another.

In the Gospel of John we read, very simply, *"I give you a new commandment, that you love one another. Just as I have loved you, you also should love one another. By this everyone will know that you are my disciples, if you have love for one another"* (John 13:34-35).

There are thousands of love songs that have been written and sung over the ages. People need love—to give love and to receive love. In this world, we can be reminded of the love of God that is ours in nature, in our family and friends, in the unexpected blessings that come to us every day, if only we are open to see them, to return love, and to make a commitment to extend the love in our corner of the world to every corner of the world.

We saw many cultures united in one millennial celebration recently. Surely, we can hold on to the possibility that this joy about our lives, this wonderful medley of song and dance, of fireworks and drumming, of silence and noise, can go on. We can be confident of our part in this almost magical symphony called life.

I ask you to try something. Begin to notice the connections between events in your life. Notice the person who shows up at just the right time. Notice the message that comes just when you need it. Notice the large or small events that might push you one way or the other at a decision point. When you need to make a decision, be open to the answers that God places before you. Affirm that the Lord will guide you to the place, the job, the relationship you seek. Keep on believing that, and doing what *you* need to do to make it happen. Trust that God will support you. Be open to the unexpected. God may have plans for you that you cannot even imagine.

You can begin whenever you choose to, wherever you are. As you begin the next phase of your journey, remember that God is with you and God blesses you richly every step of the way.

And the journey is part of the gift.

### Step 10: Make peace in the world!

Then I saw a new heaven and a new earth; for the first heaven and the first earth had passed away, and the sea was no more. And I saw the holy city, the new Jerusalem, coming down out of heaven from God, prepared as a bride adorned for her husband. And I heard a loud voice from the throne saying,

*"See, the home of God is among mortals.*
*He will dwell with them as their God;*
*they will be his peoples,*
*and God himself will be with them;*
*he will wipe every tear from their eyes.*
*Death will be no more;*
*mourning and crying and pain will be no more,*
*for the first things have passed away."*

And the one who was seated on the throne said, "See, I am making all things new." Also he said, "Write this, for these words are trustworthy and true." Then he said to me, "It is done! I am the Alpha and the Omega, the beginning and the end."

REVELATION 21:1-6a

# Worldwide Prayers for Peace

## PRAYER OF SAINT FRANCIS

*Lord, make me an instrument of your peace.*
*Where there is hatred, let me sow love;*
*Where there is injury, pardon;*
*Where there is doubt, faith;*
*Where there is despair, hope;*
*Where there is darkness, light; and*
*Where there is sadness, joy. O Divine Master,*
>     *grant that I may not so much seek to be consoled,*
>     *as to console; To be understood, as to understand;*
*To be loved, as to love. For it is in giving*
>     *that we receive—*
*It is in pardoning that we are pardoned;*
*And it is in dying that we are born to eternal life.*

ATTRIBUTED TO SAINT FRANCIS OF ASSISI, 1182-1226

## FROM THE KORAN OF ISLAM

Hold fast, all together, to God's rope, and be not divided among yourselves. Remember with gratitude God's favor on you, or you were enemies and He joined your hearts in love, so that by His grace you became brethren. Let there arise out of you one community...

QUR'AN 3.103-5

## FROM THE RIG VEDA OF HINDUISM

Meet together, speak together, let your minds be of one accord....Let your aims be common, and your hearts of one accord, and all of you be of one mind, so you may live well together.

RIG VEDA 10.191.2-4

## FROM THE SACRED WRITINGS OF THE BAHA'I FAITH

O contending peoples and kindreds of the earth! Set your faces towards unity, and let the radiance of its light shine upon you. Gather ye together, and for the sake of God resolve to root out whatever is the source of contention among you.

GLEANINGS FROM THE WRITINGS OF BAHA'U'LLAH 111

## FROM THE MISHNAH OF JUDAISM

If two sit together and the words between them are of Torah, then the Shechinah [the presence of God] is in their midst.

MISHNAH, ABOT 3.2

## FROM THE NEW TESTAMENT OF CHRISTIANITY

Every kingdom divided against itself is laid waste, and no city or house divided against itself will stand.

MATTHEW 12:25

## PEACE PRAYER OF A BUDDHIST PRIEST

O mighty lord of cosmic light. Thou art the lifegiver, sustainer, and preserver. Bless this suffering world and bestow peace in our minds. Give us strength to live in Peace and Harmony together. Banish from the face of the earth, Violence and Conflict of every kind. Transform this world into Love and Compassion for Now and All Times. O mighty lord, the sustainer and giver of life, bathe this troubled world with radiant rays of thy compassionate light.[33]

## PRAYER FOR UNITY OF FAITHS

O God, we are one with you. You have made us one with you. You have taught us that if we are open to one another, you dwell in us. Help us to preserve this openness and to fight for it with all our hearts. Help us to realize that there can be no understanding where there is mutual rejection. O God, in accepting one another wholeheartedly, fully, completely, we accept you, and we thank you, and we adore you, and we love you with our whole being, because our being is your being, our spirit is rooted in your spirit. Fill us then with love, and let us be bound together with love as we go our diverse ways, united in this one spirit which makes you present in the world, and which makes you witness to the ultimate reality that is love. Love has overcome. Love is victorious.

THOMAS MERTON (1915-1968)

## THE APOCALYPTIC VISION

Then I saw a new heaven and a new earth; for the first heaven and the first earth had passed away, and the sea was no more. And I saw the holy city, the new Jerusalem, coming down out of heaven from God, prepared as a bride adorned for her husband. And I heard a loud voice from the throne saying,

*"See, the home of God is among mortals.*
*He will dwell with them as their God;*
*they will be his peoples,*
*and God himself will be with them;*

*he will wipe every tear from their eyes.*
*Death will be no more;*
*mourning and crying and pain*
*will be no more,*
*for the first things have passed away."*

And the one who was seated on the throne said, "See, I am making all things new." Also he said, "Write this, for these words are trustworthy and true." Then he said to me, "It is done! I am the Alpha and the Omega, the beginning and the end."

REVELATION 21:1-6a

# How to Be
# a Peacemaker

## YOUR CALL, MY CALL, OUR CALL

*Scriptural Focus* ∽ *Mark 8:22-26; Luke 9:1-10*

In our journey through life, our highest calling is to get back in touch with our own God-given symphony, to live from the inside out. We need to feel the music in the deepest places of our being that God has placed in our individual hearts. It is a call to consciousness. It requires great persistence, patience and clarity. Evolution of the spirit is truly a birthing process. Just like the physical birthing process, it can bring unspeakable pains, and earth shattering joys. Yet the result of the process is worth the unpleasant parts of the journey itself.

KERRY CANNAVA[34]

How do you think you would feel if you were one of the twelve apostles, and one day Jesus blessed you and said: "Go out, cure diseases, cast out demons"? That is what Jesus did. Now it is true that, in those days, the way you learned a trade was to live and work with an expert. You were an apprentice, and your mentor, your teacher, looked over your shoulder and worked with you, day after day, until you knew as much as he could teach you. If you were meant to be a rabbi, you studied with a rabbi, and when the time was right, you went out on your own. This happened with girls, too, whose mothers taught them the homemaking skills they would need. This apprenticeship process was used in our own culture until modern times, and in some fields, like medicine, it continues.

But what about the early disciples of Jesus? How could they possibly be ready to do what Jesus did—to minister to others, to affect the lives of people and reach their hearts—after such a short time? A couple of fisherman, a tax-collector, some laborers—how prepared were they for this going forth? It's a valid point, because human nature hasn't changed all that much over time.

I imagine they were a little frightened. I imagine that they were not too sure about their ability to be like Jesus. Sure, they admired Jesus. Yes, he was their teacher and mentor, and they were together most all the time. But Jesus did extraordinary things, while they knew very well that they were very ordinary, and imperfect. Peter was always blurting out inappropriate comments. James and John fought over who was the greatest. They weren't really sure of Jesus, and seemed genuinely surprised when he rescued them from a storm at sea, when he healed the sick, when he spoke and energized the crowds.

Remember what Jesus told them when he called them to follow? "I will make you fishers of people." This mysterious analogy must have caused them fear and confusion. How? Why?

> God uses broken things. It takes broken soil to produce a crop, broken clouds to give rain, broken grain to give bread, broken bread to give strength. It is the broken alabaster box that gives forth perfume. It is Peter, weeping bitterly, who returns to greater power than ever.
>
> VANCE HAVNER[35]

So how could these men, broken and imperfect, be chosen to share the Good News? They knew Jesus. They had been touched by the call of Jesus, empowered by his power, cleansed by his mercy, and prepared by his life—his works and his words. These men were not vain. They had no idea of the influence they would have on others. They were simply doing what their master had prepared them to do, without even knowing it.

And what was their call? To make peace. To go about meeting with whomever would listen, to tell them the story. If they were accepted, they were to stay a while. And if they were rejected, they were to dust off their sandals and move on. In the deepest sense, they were to be carriers, vessels of the Good News, free to anyone who welcomed them.

When they returned from that first outing, they were full of joy and pride. They had been received with welcome arms; people were hungry for the good news they brought. They had a taste of success. And they continued to go out…and the path got more difficult.

There is a sense, of course, in which every person is called to be a peacemaker.

We are all to be witnesses, no matter what our other calling, profession, or labor. A generation ago, there was a wealthy man in the Midwest who was an outstanding Christian layman. People used to ask him what he did. He would reply, "I am a witness for Jesus Christ, but I pack pork to pay expenses." Our own apostleship differs in degree, but not in kind, from the apostleship that was given by God to Peter and James and John and the others.

DONALD GREY BARNHOUSE[36]

When he was with his disciples, Jesus taught them a great deal. He also connected with them at a very deep level. He connected with their hearts, with the center of their being. He was working with their souls, which were open to receive what he offered. Can we be like the apostles, who went out based solely on their trust in Jesus and their hearing of the Word of God as spoken by him?

I think this is important for us, as Church, when we look at our community and attempt things to help us be stronger Christians, ways to expand and intensify our experience when we invite others to join our faith community. If we want to be stronger Christians, if we want to ask others to join us, then, first and foremost, we need to know what it means to follow Jesus. We need to know Jesus.

There is a legend that recounts the return of Jesus to glory after his time on earth:

Even in heaven he bore the marks of his earthly pilgrimage, with its cruel cross and shameful death. The angel Gabriel approached him and said, "Master, you must have suffered terribly for people down there." He replied that he did. Gabriel continued: "And do they know and appreciate how much you loved them and what you did for them?" Jesus replied, "Oh, no! Not yet. Right now only a handful of people in Palestine know."

But Gabriel was perplexed. He asked, "Then what have you done to let everyone know about your love for them?" Jesus said, "I've asked Peter, James, John, and a few more friends to tell others about me. Those who are told will tell others, in turn, about me. And my story will be spread to the farthest reaches of the globe. Ultimately, all of humankind will have heard about my life and what I have done."

Gabriel frowned and looked rather skeptical. He well knew what poor stuff people were made of. He said, "Yes, but what if Peter and James and John grow weary? What if the people who come after them forget? What if way down in the twentieth century people just don't tell others about you? Haven't you made any other plans?"

And Jesus answered, "I haven't made any other plans. I'm counting on them."

Twenty centuries later, he still has no other plan.[37]

Jesus is counting on you and me. The early disciples devoted themselves to reaching the world. Christ counted on them, and they delivered. Have we done as well?

Beloved, let us love one another, because love is from God; everyone who loves is born of God and knows God. Whoever does not love does not know God, for God is love. God's love was revealed among us in this way: God sent his only Son into the world so that we might live through him. In this is love, not that we loved God but that he loved us and sent his Son to be the atoning sacrifice for our sins. Beloved, since God loved us so much, we also ought to love one another.

1 JOHN 4:7-11

# Epilogue

## SIX STEPS FOR *KEEPING* THE PEACE

### 1. LISTEN

*If I do not want what you want, please try not to tell me that my want is wrong.*

*Or if I believe other than you, at least pause before you correct my view.*

*Or if my emotion is less than yours, or more, given the same circumstances, try not to ask me to feel more strongly or weakly.*

*Or yet if I act, or fail to act, in the manner of your design for action, let me be. I do not, for the moment at least, ask you to understand me. That will only come when you are willing to give up changing me into a copy of you.*

*I may be your spouse, your parent, your offspring, your friend, or your colleague. If you will allow me any of my own wants, or emotions, or beliefs, or actions, then you open yourself, so that someday these ways of mine might not seem so wrong, and might finally appear to you as right—for me. To put up with me is the first step to understanding me. Not that you embrace my ways as right for you, but that you are no longer irritated or disappointed with me for my seeming way-wardness. And in understanding me you might come to prize my differences from you, and far from seeking to change me, preserve and even nurture those differ-ences.*[38]

## 2. UNDERSTAND

Peace can never be kept by force, it can only be achieved through understanding.

ALBERT EINSTEIN

## 3. SPEAK KINDLY

Kind words can be short and easy to speak, but their echoes are truly endless.

MOTHER TERESA

## 4. LIFT UP YOUR ATTITUDE

*Teach me to understand and grow and never look back into the darkness of the past, but ahead to Your ever-lasting light. Teach me to believe in myself, and that I am worthy of love; though my body may be twisted by mortal flaw, I am perfect in Your eyes. Teach me how to be an angel, so that I can better understand how to be human.*[39]

## 5. BE A BLESSING TO OTHERS

*Blessed are they who give without expecting even thanks in return, for they shall be abundantly rewarded. Blessed are they who translate every good thing they know into action, for ever higher truths shall be revealed unto them.*

*Blessed are they who do God's will without asking to see results, for great shall be their recompense.*

*Blessed are they who love and trust their fellow beings, for they shall reach the good in people and receive a loving response.*

*Blessed are they who have seen reality, for they know that not the garment of clay but that which activates the garment of clay is real and indestructible.*

*Blessed are they who see the change we call death as a liberation from the limitation of this earth-life, for they shall rejoice with their loved ones who make the glorious transition.*

*Blessed are they who, after dedicating their lives and thereby receiving a blessing, have the courage and faith to surmount the difficulties of the path ahead, for they shall receive a second blessing.*

*Blessed are they who advance toward the spiritual path without the selfish motive of seeking inner peace, for they shall find it.*

*Blessed are they who, instead of trying to batter down the gates of the kingdom of heaven, approach them humbly and lovingly and purified, for they shall pass right through.*

PEACE PILGRIM[40]

## 6. PRAY

*Eternal One, you invite us to the banquet where God reigns. You invite us to share in the sweet wine and warm bread of community. You invite us to expect and to recognize miracles where charity and love prevail. O God, you challenge us to heed your call for love and justice in community. Inspire in us the strength to seek change and the courage to embrace that change when it comes. God, may our journey move us from the injustice of past centuries to a future of reconciliation with one another and with you. Amen*

# Endnotes

1. Peace Pilgrim, *Peace Pilgrim: Her Life and Work in Her Own Words. On her pilgrimage from January 1, 1953 till July 7, 1981.* Santa Fe, NM: Ocean Tree Books, 1995, p. 72.
2. Ruth Graham Bell, *Prodigals and Those Who Love Them.* New York, NY: Baker/Revell, 1999, p. 44.
3. Mrs. Charles Cowman, "One Day at a Time." Quoted by Rev. Herman Kroeker in *A Lift For Living: A Daily Devotional,* January 30, 2000. St. Catharines, Ontario, Canada. Online resource, http://people.becon.org/~hkroeker.
4. Tom Barrett, 2000. Online resource www.interluderetreat.com/meditate/group.htm.
5. Author unknown, from "Why Worry?" at The Rainbow Garden: Personal Stories, online resource, www.io.com/~rga/personal6.html.
6. Tom Barrett, 2000. Online resource, www.interluderetreat.com/meditate/calmmind.htm.
7. Henri Nouwen, *Life of the Beloved: Spiritual Living in a Secular World.* New York, NY: Crossroad Publishing, 1992, p. 63.
8. Thich Nhat Hanh, "Walking into the Kingdom of God." Dharma Talk given in Plum Village, France, August 6, 1997, online resource www.plumvillage.org.
9. *Book of Worship: United Church of Christ.* New York, NY: United Church of Christ Office for Church Life and Leadership, 1986, p. 38.
10. James S. Hewett, *Illustrations Unlimited.* Wheaton, IL: Tyndale House Publishers, Inc., 1988, p. 218.
11. Frederick Buechner, *Listening To Your Life: Meditations with Frederick Buechner.* New York, NY: HarperCollins, 1992, p. 57.

12. Erma Bombeck, *Forever, Erma.* Quoted in <u>Reader's Digest</u>, March, 1997, p. 148.

13. Sam Levinson, *Anything But Money.* New York, NY: Simon & Schuster, 1949, 1966, p. 201.

14. Anthony de Mello, SJ, "Meaning: A Meditation by Anthony de Mello, SJ." Online resource www.elsajoy.com/spiritus8.html.

15. Pope Paul VI, online resource <u>www.religioustolerance.org/quotes1.htm</u>.

16. Arthur Schopenhauer, *Memories, Dreams, Reflections.* London: Vintage Books, 1961, p. 69.

17. Rev. Edward Hamilton, "Charting a course for new life in Jesus Christ." Online resource <u>www.morningstarchurch.org/sermons/forgiveus.html</u>.

18. Dwight Moody, *Moody's Anecdotes.* New York, NY: Baker/Revell, 1996, p. 53.

19. Oriah Mountain Dreamer, *The Invitation.* HarperSanFrancisco, 1999, "Introduction."

20. Norman Vincent Peale, online resource <u>www.aaronscollection.com/quotes/quotes.htm</u>.

21. Richard Cardinal Cushing, "Inspiration University." Online resource <u>www.angelfire.com/nv/InspirationUniv/quotes/9.html</u>.

22. Joan Borysenko, *Minding the Body, Mending the Mind.* New York, NY: Bantam, 1988, p. 10.

23. Joel Goldsmith, "Major Principles of the Infinite Way" in *The Seeker.* Perth, Australia, 1958. Online resource <u>www.abo.fi/comprel/joel.htm</u>.

24. Quoted in *Wit and Wisdom*, as submitted by Terry Galan, October 26, 2001. Online resource <u>www.witandwisdom.org/archive/20019026.htm</u>.

25. Quoted from *Los Angeles Times*, November 3, 1997. Online resource <u>www.latimes.com/archives</u>.

26. B. Scott and B. Russell. Online resource <u>http://lyrics.coolfreepages.com/Lyrics/1970/621970.html</u>.

27. Steve Ely, "To Help and Support," YouthQuest International online resource <u>www.iphc.org/cem/aoa/studies/11.html</u>.

28. John Donne, "Meditation XVII" in *Devotions Upon Emergent Occasions.* London: Vintage Spiritual Classics, 1624, p. 27.

29. Ken Kalb. Online resource, <u>www.lightshift.com/Inspiration/chapter.html</u>.

30. Ibid.

31. Related in *Wit and Wisdom*, April 30, 1999. Online resource, www.witandwisdom.org/archive/19990430.htm.

32. James S. Hewett, *Illustrations Unlimited*. Wheaton, IL: Tyndale House Publishers, 1988, pp. 233-34.

33. Found online at www.interluderetreat.com/meditate/paxnwar.htm.

34. Kerry Cannava, excerpted from "Inner Evolution…Transforming Your Life From the Inside Out," 2001, online at www.embracingyour-spirit.com.

35. Vance Havner, "Broken Things," online resource http://sofinesjoyfulmoments.com/mstrstch/broken.htm.

36. Quoted by Dayton Burt, "Go Ye!" a sermon. Online resource www.sermons.org/sermons/sermon43.html.

37. Visda Point: Center for Christian Education and Service, online resource www.geocities.com/visdapoint/mtpintro.html.

38. Author unknown. From "The Story Bin" online resource www.storybin.com/wisdom/wisdom112.shtml.

39. Spiritual Sisters.com of the Internet Café. Online resource, May 25, 2001, www.spiritualsisters.com/page130.htm.

40. Peace Pilgrim, "Peace Pilgrim's Beatitudes," in *Friends of Peace Pilgrim*. Manuscript copyright 1982, 1991, E-book copyright 1999, Boris Acosta, APPENDIX IV, p. 4.

# About the Author

Mary E. Latela has an Master's of Divinity degree from Yale University. She is currently an instructor at several colleges in Connecticut. She is a certified pastoral counselor and long-time Liguori author whose most recent titles are *Healing the Abusive Family: Beyond Survival* and *Prepare Him Room: Advent For Busy Christians.*